DATE			
7·22			

A Garland Series

The Feminist Controversy
in England 1788-1810

A collection of 44 interesting
and important works reprinted
in photo-facsimile in 89 volumes

edited by

Gina Luria

Rutgers University

Plans of Education

With Remarks on the Systems of Other Writers

Clara <u>Reeve</u>

with an introduction
for the Garland edition by
Gina Luria

Garland Publishing, Inc., New York & London

1974

*LC
1421
.R49
1974*

Cop. 1

Bibliographical note:

This facsimile has been made from a copy in the
British Museum
(8311.a.1)

Library of Congress Cataloging in Publication Data

Reeve, Clara, 1729-1807.
   Plans of education.

   (The Feminist controversy in England, 1788-1810)
   Reprint of the 1792 ed. printed for T. Hookham and
J. Carpenter, London.
   1. Education of women.   2. Education--Philosophy.
I. Title.   II.   Series.
LC1421.R49   1974   376   73-22215
ISBN 0-8240-0877-4

Printed in the United States of America

Introduction

Clara Reeve (1729-1807) was born at Ipswich, the daughter of a minister. While still quite young she was tutored by her father who had her read parliamentary debates, English history, and the classics. Her first literary attempt was a translation of a Latin romance, published in 1772 as *The Phoenix*. Her second, and most successful, work was a novel, *The Champion of Virtue, a Gothic Story* (1777). It was afterwards known as *The Old English Baron*. Reeve's essay, *The Progress of Romance* (1785; reprint edition, N.Y.: Garland Publishing, 1971), offers an instructive discussion of the fiction of the 1770s and 1780s. Always responsive to the tastes of the time, Reeve's *Plans of Education, with Remarks on the Systems of Other Writers* (1792) is evidence of the contemporary concern over the questions of woman's place and women's rights. Published in the same year as Mary Wollstonecraft's militant *Vindication*

of the Rights of Woman, Plans of Education reveals
an acceptance of precisely those widely held prejudices against a "rational" life for women to which
Wollstonecraft and the English feminists of the
1790s addressed themselves.

Gina Luria

Select Bibliography

Reeve, Clara. *The Old English Baron, with a memoir of the
author by Sir Walter Scott.* London: Ballantyne's
Novelists' Library, 1821.

PLANS OF EDUCATION.

PLANS OF EDUCATION;

WITH

R E M A R K S

ON THE

SYSTEMS OF OTHER WRITERS.

IN A SERIES OF LETTERS BETWEEN

MRS. DARNFORD AND HER FRIENDS.

BY CLARA REEVE.

Train up a Child in the Way he should go, and when he is old he will not depart from it.

PROVERBS OF SOLOMON.

L O N D O N:

PRINTED FOR T. HOOKHAM, AND J. CARPENTER, NEW AND OLD BOND-STREET,

1792.

P R E F A C E.

IT feems to me that fome kind of apology may be neceffary for offering the following fheets to the eye of the public.

The fubjects of them have been of late years inveftigated by many writers of abilities and knowledge, far fuperior to mine; it is neverthelefs true, that the fame fubject may be differently treated by various writers; that they have each taken different parts of it; and every one may have ftarted fomething new, and treated it in a manner peculiar to himfelf.

I beg leave to obferve alfo, that moft of the particulars to be found here, lie fcattered and difperfed in many authors, which are now bound up together;

gether; they may fpare much trouble to thofe who would not take the pains to fearch for them; and expence to thofe who cannot purchafe many books upon this fubject; who yet may eafily get at this little work, and, perhaps, may find in it the fub-ftance of many others, contracted into a fmall compafs.

The importance of the fubject may be thought by many to make its apology, for thofe who are defirous to offer the fruits of their labour and ex-perience, from an ardent wifh of promoting the good of fociety, and leffening evils caufed by indo-lent and bad members of it. Thefe motives may deferve excufe, where they are not entitled to ap-plaufe.

Moft of thefe Plans were written many years ago. I had wifhed to collect them together, and to add fuch remarks as have arifen to my mind. Since I have done this, I have feen feveral new Plans, of which I had not the leaft knowledge; particularly, the fcheme of the Philanthropic So-ciety,

ciety, and the account of the Shrewfbury Houfe
of Induftry. I rejoice to fee that there is a fpirit
of reformation arifen among us, and hope it will
proceed, and be effectual to the whole body of the
common people of this land, which does exceedingly ftand in need of it. The numbers of them
that are put to death, and thofe fent abroad to diftant fettlements, are melancholy proofs of this un-
welcome truth.

I do not prefume to trace the fources of thefe
evils; they lie too deep for me to prefume to fa-
thom. May thofe whofe duty it is to watch over
the welfare and morals of the people, difcover
and reform them, while it is yet in their power!

I have feen Mrs. Macauly Graham's Letters on
Education, in which there are many fine things,
and many ferious truths; but it does not interfere
with my defign, which is to fimplify my fubjects;
and my method of treating them, to reduce them
to the ftandard of common fenfe, and within the
limits of practicability. I do not prefume to med-
dle

dle with metaphyſical ſpeculations. " Such knowledge is too wonderful for me ; I cannot attain
unto it ;" but plain reaſoning, and remarks drawn
from ſcenes that have paſſed before my eyes in my
journey through life, theſe are what I humbly preſent to my readers, hoping they may not be deemed
unworthy to ſtand upon the ſhelf, among the works
of other ſcribblers of this reading and writing
age.

PLANS

PLANS

OF

EDUCATION.

LETTER I.

LADY A———, TO MRS. DARNFORD.

A SERIES of great and important events have engaged my attention for two years paſt, and hindered my writing to dear Mrs. Darnford, as I have many times intended to do. I will not expatiate on my paſt ſufferings, nor revive painful recollections to you and myſelf; it is ſufficient to ſay they are paſt, and that fairer proſpects are opened to me.

I came over to ſettle the affairs of my-

B   ſelf

felf and my children ; this bufinefs was
out of my way, and above my abilities :
in Lord A——, I have found a faithful
friend and protector; and I thought I
could not do better than to put myfelf
and children under his care, and give
him a right and title to be the firft friend
of us all. I believe and truft I fhall never
have caufe to repent it.

I have often been journeying between
London and Lord A——'s feat in B——
fhire, and when in the capital, I have made
enquiries after you.—I was told that you
had a fifter in the city ; I found her out
and queftioned her ; fhe gave a very con-
fufed and imperfect account of you, and
I could perceive that fhe did not favour
you. She blamed you exceedingly for
giving up your fettlement ; I admired and
praifed you for it. She faid you went out,
after Mr. Darnford's death, as governefs
to fome young ladies ; that you expected

fo

fo much attention, that nobody could pleafe you; and after trying feveral families, you left London, and fet up a day-fchool in a little country town. That in two years time you grew tired of that, and went to the houfe of a fea-captain, who went abroad, and left the care of his houfe and his wife to you. That the woman was out of her fenfes, and the houfe reputed to be haunted. That you were there ftill for aught fhe knew to the contrary, and fhe knew nothing more. This account was by no means fatisfactory to me, but I waited till my next trip to London for further information.

Luckily for me, I met at the houfe of an acquaintance, a friend of yours, called Mrs. Langfton, and fhe gave me the information I wanted; fhe fhewed me the right fide of the medal.

Good God!—How ftrange the different reprefentation of the fame facts and cir-

cumftances!

cumſtances!—How honourable for you
was Mrs. Langſton's relation of your adventures, and at the ſame time how true.
She wiſhed to have your company; ſhe
complained of you; but it was like a
lover who is grieved and mortified that
another is preferred before himſelf. *That*
Mrs. Strictland, who claims the firſt place
in your affections. *That* Donna Iſabella
di Soranzo, who owes you the greateſt of
all obligations. You muſt tell me every
thing that relates to yourſelf and your ſituation. I am contriving to put you into a
way of doing this, without the trouble of
writing a new relation of all your adventures.

Mrs. Langſton ſays you have promiſed
to viſit her next winter; after this you cannot refuſe me a ſhare of your company;
for though not the oldeſt friend, I preſume
to ſay, you have not a more ſincere, nor
yet a more affectionate one.

From

From the firſt day I ſaw you I was in-
tereſted in your fate ; your conduct in
every trying fituation has increaſed my
regard for you, and my defire to engage
your friendſhip and company.

I am bleſſed with four fine children,
two of each ſex. My eldeſt ſon is placed
at Eton, the younger at a nurſery ſchool.

I have a great defire to educate my
daughters at home ; I wiſh to engage a
governeſs for them, that I can make my
ſubſtitute, and rely upon her care and
fidelity. There is ſuch a one in your
knowledge, and I implore your intereſt
with her.

The lady with whom you have refided
lately, is quite reſtored to health of body
and mind, as Mrs. Langſton informs
me.

Your other friend has ſettled her houſe-
hold, and can ſpare you. Cannot you give
me your company and affiſtance in the

arduous

arduous tafk of female education? I fhould look upon you as my fifter and my friend, and think all the obligation is on my fide. I have afked my lord's opinion on this fubject. He anfwered me: " If Mrs. Darnford has no objection, I can have none."

Confider my dear Madam of my pro-pofal and fend me your, anfwer as foon as you have determined.

I am, dear Mrs. Darnford,

Your truly affectionate friend,

L—— A——.

LETTER

LETTER II.

MRS. DARNFORD TO LADY A———.

I AM inexpreffibly obliged to your Ladyfhip for your generous rememberance of fo obfcure a perfon as Frances Darnford. I can never forget the favours I have received from your unmerited bounties; and the proofs of your efteem and friendfhip warm my heart as often as I refleɛt upon them.

I have been fo particularly circumftanced, as to be obliged to decline thofe offers of proteɛtion and patronage, which it would have been my pleafure and my pride to accept, had I been at liberty to do fo; but I was detained by indifpenfible duties, which had I not obeyed, would have been a reproach to my mind at this hour; yet to your ladyfhip, might, at that time, have appeared

B 4 like

like ingratitude. Thofe duties and obligations are now diffolved; but new ones
have arifen that have claimed my time
and my fervices.

I was for more than two years engaged
in the office of tuition; I applied fo
clofely that my health fuffered, and I accepted an offer to take the care of Madame di Soranzo, who was at that time in
an unhappy ftate of health, both of body
and mind; partly from the grief for the
lofs of her hufband, and partly from ap-
prehended dangers of other kinds. Captain Maurice had brought her from Italy
with her hufband; he took upon him
the office of her friend and protector.—
He wifhed to marry her, and his folicita-
tions increafed her diforder. This gentleman had placed under my care, a young
lady, his relation, to whom he was guardian; being pleafed with my behaviour
towards her, he wifhed me to take Donna
                                    Ifabella

Isabella under my care also. I was so happy as to succeed in the discharge of my duty to both. Donna Isabella was restored to perfect health; she contracted an attachment to me, and we promised an eternal and inviolable friendship for each other.

She believes my company necessary to her happiness; she loves all those that are dear to me. My ward, Miss Brady, lives with us, as does also an adopted child of mine, and they all look up to me as their friend, steward, and manager; in short, they would all be made unhappy if I were to leave them.

I have the pleasure to inform your Ladyship, that I am competently provided for, and with prudent care am out of the reach of poverty. My excellent friend, Counsellor M——, put out my monies for me, and taught me to make my little fortune accumulate; at his death he left

me

me five hundred pounds; a noble legacy, but not able to compenfate for the lofs of an ineftimable friend.

Captain Maurice was exceedingly generous to me; he intrufted to my care the intereft of Mifs Brady's fortune, and appointed me his fteward, to receive and employ the rents of an eftate of his. I have taken to myfelf annually as much as I thought due to me for Mifs Brady's education and board; the remainder I have fet apart, and fhall account for it to Captain Maurice.

Since I have lived with Madame di Soranzo, I have been free of all expences; fhe will not even fuffer me to pay her for the board of Mifs Brady and Patty Martin. All this time my own property has been accumulating; fo that I can truly fay (with ardent thanks to the Almighty for all his bleffings) I am as rich and as independent as I wifh to be.

Mrs.

Mrs. Strictland was my fchool-fellow and the friend of my youth. After fhe became a widow, fhe wrote to me, and urged me to come and affift her in the education of her daughter; fhe made me the moft noble and generous offers, and was not pleafed with my declining them, till I had convinced her, that I was engaged in the fervice of others, who had more need of me. I related my whole hiftory to her; I alfo told her that of Donna Ifabella di Soranzo. She is now fatisfied with me, and our friendfhip is knit more ftrongly than ever.

She has made a vifit to my friend, and engaged her friendfhip. We are now returning it; and fhe is very unwilling to part with us, but would fain have us winter at Woodlands.

I am under a promife to fpend fome time with Mrs. Langfton. Mrs. Strictland wifhes me to leave Madame di So-

ranzo,

ranzo, and my two children, with her
till my return. I am now confidering
this point, and have not yet determined.
From what I have faid, your Ladyfhip will
judge of my fituation, and of my obligation to remain in it. I hope you will not
be offended at my declining your kind
propofal, and that you will believe I am
extremely fenfible of the honour you have
done me. What then can I do to fhew
my fenfe of all your goodnefs to me? I
am ftudying to do this, and to deferve
the honour of your friendfhip and correfpondence, and at leaft to offer you
my poor fervices, to the extent of my
ability.

During the time that I was contending
with poverty at a diftance, and perceiving
that his nearer approach was inevitable, I
employed and amufed myfelf with forming Plans of Education. I read all the
beft books of the kind, and confidered the
good

good and bad effects of them. I perceived marks of imperfection in them all,
but imputed them to the caufe that attends all human fyftems, framed by imperfect creatures.—Yet again, I reflected
that all knowledge is progreffive; and in
tracing the errors of former writers, we
advance ftep by ftep towards perfection,
but never need fear approaching too near
it.

If I fhould be fo fortunate to ftrike out
any new lights upon this important fubject, or fet old ones in a new or more
practicable one, I fhall have difcharged
the duties of a good citizen of the world,
and I fhall think I have not lived for no
purpofe.

Your Ladyfhip is folicitous to inform
yourfelf, and to inftruct thofe whom God
has committed to your care, in the beft
manner. You have defired my affiftance;
by communicating my ideas to you, I
fhall

shall do all in my power to promote your laudable intentions. I will transcribe and revise these papers, and send them to your Ladyship, and shall request the favour of receiving your remarks upon them; by this means we may each receive benefit from the other; and perhaps I may be enabled to be of some service to you;—the only return I can ever make for your generous and disinterested friendship.

While I am thus employed, I shall beg of Mrs. Strictland to give my young pupils leave to make extracts from her letters and mine, of all that has befallen me ever since your Ladyship went abroad, down to the time that I entered into the service of Madame di Soranzo. I shall desire Mrs. Strictland to mark the passages they are to transcribe, and to superintend their writing. This will be an exercise of their pen, and an improvement also; by

tranfcribing,

tranfcribing, they will, in due time learn
to compofe.

If the recital of my adventures fhould
not tire your Ladyfhip, I will endeavour
to prevail on Madame di Soranzo, to permit me to relate hers alfo, which are to
be found in my letters to Mrs. Strictland;
and I will afk leave of this lady to give
you the Memoirs of the family of Marney, which fhe has been inftrumental in
reftoring from poverty and diftrefs, to
competence and happinefs. Thefe communications will furnifh fufficient fubjects
for our future correfpondence, they will
prove my refpect and gratitude to your
Ladyfhip, and procure me, as I hope, the
return of your letters, and remarks upon
all the fubjects I have mentioned.

If I have been too prefumptuous in my
expectations, it is in your Ladyfhip's
power to check me; or, if you approve
them,

them, to encourage me. I wait for your next as the criterion.

With the warmeſt wiſhes for your happineſs, and of all thoſe who are near and dear to you,

I am, Madam,

Your Ladyſhip's moſt obedient ſervant,

FRANCES DARNFORD.

LETTER

L E T T E R · III.

LADY A———, TO MRS. DARNFORD.

DEAR MRS. DARNFORD,

I OWE you many thanks for your obliging letter, which has afforded me
matter for much reflection, and has pro-
duced fome effects wholly unforefeen by
you or me; which, upon the whole, have
given me much fatisfaction.

The reafons you affigned for declining
my propofal, were quite fufficient to acquit you to me; but another has been dif-
clofed fince, which might perhaps to you
be the ftrongeft of all.

My Lord allows me to tell you of a
converfation which paffed between him
and me upon the fubject of your letter,
as a proof of his honour and fincerity
towards us both.

When

When I received your letter, I told
my lord of it. He coloured and fmiled.
" Tell me, Madam, does Mrs. Darnford accept the charge of your daughters ?" " No, my Lord, fhe declines it,
but in a very handfome manner." He
laughed—" I knew it—I was fure of it."
" My lord, you faid, you had no objection, if Mrs. Darnford had none ?" " So
I did ; but I was certain fhe would raife
objections." " Then I fuppofe your
lordfhip can account for them ?" " Will
you permit me to read her letter, Lady
A——— ?" " With all my heart, my lord,
here it is."—(He read it attentively.)—
" Very well ; fhe has declined your offer
handfomely ; but fhe had a ftronger reafon in referve, than any fhe has mentioned." " I prefume you would not
have excited my curiofity, unlefs you intended to gratify it ?" " You are right,
Madam ;

Madam; I think it due to your merit,
and to Mrs. Darnford's.—You fhall know,
then, that I made her an offer to be my
wife of the left hand, and I thought I
did her an honour at the time; but I have
fince come to a better way of thinking,
and I refpect her for her refufal." " How
did fhe receive it, my Lord?" " With
pride and refolution.—She obliged me to
turn my eye inward, and to fee what I
did not like in myfelf. I called her proud,
faucy, and impertinent!—fhe was cool
and fteady; yet, I verily believe, that had
fhe treated me kindly, fhe had been at
this moment in your place, Lady A——;
but 1 was affronted by her behaviour; I
had reafon to think fhe had a rooted dif-
like to me; my pride rofe againft her,
and I was cured; but it coft me much
pain, for I did love her truly." " But
you forgive her now, my lord, and refpect

ſpect her the more ?"　" I do reſpect her;
but I feel at times ſomething like re-
ſentment, which I will endeavour to ſub-
due."　" You have no objection to my
keeping up a correſpondence with Mrs.
Darnford ?"　" Certainly not; I believe
it will be an advantage to you both.——
Ever ſince I gave my vows to you, I re-
ſolved to fulfil all the duties I have
taken upon me; and I hope what I have
ſaid, will be a proof of my honour and
ſincerity towards you both."　" It is, indeed, my lord, and I thank you for the
confidence you have ſhewn me : I will
ſtudy to deſerve it."

" It is I that muſt ſtudy to deſerve your
affection and confidence. I have been free
in my conduct while a ſingle man, but as
a married one, you ſhall have no cauſe to
complain of me.

" When you anſwer this letter, give
my

my compliments to Mrs. Darnford, tell her, I rejoice to hear fhe is competently provided for.—I will never again affront her by offering my fervices ; but, I hope, fhe will always rely upon your friendfhip."

Here ended our converfation on this fubject. I have obeyed my lord's orders, and complied with my own inclinations, in communicating it to you. Thus authorifed, I demand your friendfhip and confidence.

I thankfully embrace your offer of fending me your Plans of Education, and your remarks upon this fubject ; and alfo your communications relative to yourfelf and your friends.

They will be extremely acceptable to me ; I expect information and improvement from them ; and I will make you fuch returns as I am enabled to do from time to time.

Pray

Pray make me known to your friends; prefent my compliments and good wifhes to them, and tell them they muft love me in return, as your moft affectionate friend and fervant,

L—— A——.

LETTER

LETTER IV.

MRS. DARNFORD TO LADY A——.

AGAIN I acknowledge the honour done me in Lady A——'s friend-ship and correspondence. I beg you to return my thanks to Lord A—— for giving his permiſſion; and for his good wiſhes reſpecting myſelf; may he long enjoy the bleſſings heaven has given him, with a due ſenſe of their value and of his own happineſs!

I am now putting my papers together, in order to render my correſpondence of ſome value; and ſhall enter upon the ſub-ject I have promiſed to inveſtigate.

ESSAY

E S S A Y

O N

EDUCATION AND MANNERS.

————

IN the morning of life, when youth
are firſt engaged in worldly purſuits and
expeſtations, in the warmth of their hearts
they find every thing around them in the
right place.

All they ſee is beautiful, all they hear
is delightful ; the ſociety they mix with is
the moſt agreeable, the country they were
born in is the firſt in the world,; its government and manners the moſt perfeſt.
—As they advance in their progreſs, experience draws back the veil that blinded
them, and ſhews them the defeſts of all
thoſe things they once admired. When
they have reached the top of the hill, they
ſtand ſtill and reflect upon them ; they

compare

compare things paſt with the preſent, and look forward to the future with doubt and fuſpicion; but in this ſtate they are moſt likely to judge truly and impartially.

As they deſcend the hill, they grow more diſſatisfied and querulous; they grow partial to the time of their youth, when their paſſions were moſt awakened, and their enjoyments the moſt lively and engaging.

Thus the young and the old throw contempt upon each other, and each of them have enough to ſay in juſtification of their own opinions. The affected wiſdom and garrulity of age, is a conſtant ſubject of ridicule to youth; and ſerves them as a touchſtone to ſharpen their wit upon.

‘ My grand-mother told me, what her grand-mother told her,
‘ The times grow worſer child, as they grow older.’

“ Oh,

" Oh, God-a-mercy times!—If this were true,
" What would another century dwindle to ?—
" I dare maintain this time as good as any,
" In fpite of whiners, grumblers, or my granny."

Epilogue to a Dramatic Caricature, called, Tafte and Feeling.

This is the conftant language of igno-rance, pertnefs, and folly ; but to the many it may, feem like wit, poetry, and even truth. This falfe idea is the fource of a thoufand errors and vices. If things ftand ftill, and grow neither better nor worfe, why fhould we give ourfelves any concern about times or manners ?

A fecond inference is, that if all things are right, they can have nothing to re-form ; we are then as good as we need to be, and it is only peevifh, melancholy, and querulous people who find fault ; becaufe it gives vent to their fpleen and ill-nature. Neither times nor people want any amend-ment, and we refolve neither to amend the times, nor ourfelves.

But

But let us liften to the man of reafon and reflection, who ftands at the top of the hill, and attend to his obfervations and inferences :

> " Let me not live," (fays he,).
> " After my flame lacks oil, to be the fnuff .
> " Of younger fpirits, whofe apprehenfive fenfe
> " All but new things difdain :—whofe judgments
>   are
> " Mere fathers of their garments, — whofe con-
>   ftancies
> " Expire before their fafhions."

SHAKESPEARE.

Let us examine into the truth of thefe opinions refpectively. Hiftory and experience inform us that all fublunary things are in an eternal rotation : ftates and kingdoms, arts and fciences, languages and manners, all are fubject to perpetual viciffitudes. Who dares affirm that any thing ftands ftill, when the world itfelf, and all that it contains, are in continual motion ?

When a nation is in a ftate of civilization, there is a gradation by which it afcends to the higheſt degree of cultivation; when the language and manners, arts and ſciences, are in the greateſt perfection—refinement upon theſe ſucceeds; refinement becomes faſtidious, wanton, effeminate. Falſe taſte and affectation ſucceed relaxation in manners and diſcipline; all theſe deſcend and decline, till in procefs of time, they return to ignorance and barbariſm.

It is worthy of obſervation, that the manners and the language of a people have generally kept in the ſame ſtate of ſtrength and weakneſs. When the arts and ſciences have attained their higheſt ſummit; when the manners were poliſhed and yet virtuous; the language alſo has been in the higheſt perfection. As the manners became corrupt and effeminate, the language alſo degenerated, and both ſunk together.

Education

Education is the fource from whence manners proceed; when this is fimple and virtuous, the effects are feen plainly; when the fountain is poifoned, the ftreams are polluted, and all who drank of them are diftempered and infected.

Nothing is of equal confequence to the health of a ftate, as the education of youth. When the manners are chafte and virtuous, we cannot doubt that education was fo; when there is a general relaxation of manners and difcipline, there muft be great defects in the methods of education.

Philofophers fet themfelves to work to inveftigate the caufes of this declenfion; they frame new fyftems of education.— They are like old Thales, the Milefian, who, while he was gazing at the ftars, over-looked the pit that was under his feet; he ftumbled and fell into it.

In

In order to underſtand clearly the ob-
ject of our reſearch, we muſt throw aſide
all abſtract reaſoning, and metaphyſical
ſubtleties; we muſt ſimplify every thing,
and bring back our ideas to nature, truth,
and right reaſon.

Let us then enquire into one great
point, upon which all our reaſoning muſt
depend.—Ought children to be governed
by diſcipline, or left to educate themſelves?—Are they to be reſtrained very
ſtrongly,—very gently,—or not at all?—
I am not going to ſet up for a ſyſtem-
maker, I ſhall only remark upon the
ſyſtems of others, according to my
own judgment. — In the firſt place I
ſhall enquire what were the opinions of
the ancients, upon the ſubject of education.

I will begin this enquiry with the Sa-
cred Writings, as they ought to have the
greateſt

greateſt weight with us who profeſs to believe them.

Solomon was highly celebrated for his wiſdom; he adviſes that children ſhould be reſtrained very ſtrongly, as appears by the following extracts from the Proverbs, aſcribed to him:

" Folly is bound up in the heart of a child, and the rod of correction muſt drive it out.

" He that ſpareth the rod hateth his ſon; but he that loveth him chaſteneth him betimes.

" Chaſten thy ſon while there is hope, and let not thy ſoul ſpare for his crying.

" Correct thy ſon and he ſhall give thee reſt; yea, he ſhall give delight unto thy ſoul.

" The rod and reproof give wiſdom: but a child left to himſelf bringeth his parents to ſhame."

There are many other Proverbs to the ſame effect, but theſe may ſuffice for the preſent purpoſe.

The ſon of Sirach, in his admirable work, which is juſtly called Wiſdom; has this remarkable paſſage:

" Haſt

" Haſt thou children ?—Inſtruct them, and bow down
their necks from their youth.

" Haſt thou daughters ?—Have a care of their bodies,
and ſhew not thyſelf chearful towards them.

I will preſume to paraphraſe theſe ſen-
tences, as they may at the firſt view appear
too harſh and ſevere.

Haſt thou ſons ?—Subject them to ſtrict diſcipline, and
keep them in due ſubjection to their parents and
preceptors.

Haſt thou daughters ?—Watch over their behaviour
with unremitting care and ſtrict attention; and
do not accuſtom thyſelf to be too familiar with
them, left they loſe the reſpect that they owe thee
as their parent.

Thus much is ſufficient to ſhew the
opinions of the Jews on this head.

I cannot forbear citing a paſſage of St.
Paul, which ſtrongly corroborates thoſe
above recited.

" If we are chaſtiſed, God dealeth with us as ſons;
for what ſon is he whom his father chaſteneth not.

He ſuppoſes that no parent can love his
child, unleſs he correct him; and alſo
that this was a generally received truth.

The

The ancient Perſians educated their youth with great ſtrictneſs, and even ſeverity; the young nobility were inured to all kinds of hardſhips and fatigues; hunting and military exerciſes were their conſtant uſe.

They were taught to deſpiſe danger and death for the love of their country, and to avoid all thoſe pleaſures that emaſculate the mind, and enervate the body. They were taught to obey their teachers implicitly, in order to qualify them to command.

The Greeks made the education of their youth a principal part of their polity: all the different ſtates kept their youth in ſtrict ſubjection; but the ſeverity of the Spartan diſcipline is well known to have exceeded all others.

The ancient Romans had an abſolute power over the lives of their children;

they

they kept them at the greateſt diſtance, and by ſlow degrees admitted them to familiarity with themſelves.

A celebrated Greek writer obſerves, that there were more undutiful children among his countrymen, than among the Romans; becauſe with the former, the power over their children expired when they came of age; and with the latter, it remained in full force afterwards.

It is worthy of our particular obſervation; that when the Romans declined from the virtues and ſimplicity of their anceſtors, they likewiſe relaxed in the ſeverity of their education; by degrees they grew negligent of this important duty, the formations of the minds and manners of their youth.

When they were at the meridian of their power, riches, and luxury; they be-

came

came folicitous to educate them to polite
literature and manners; but in regard to
great and manly virtues they grew care-
lefs and indifferent.

While the Roman youth were learning
the language and eloquence of the Gre-
cian fophifts, Cato the Cenfor earneftly
declaimed againft them; he advifed the
Senate to fend them back to their own
country: "Left our youth," faid he,
" fhould learn to prefer the glory of
fpeaking to that of acting well."

Cato foretold the confequences that actually followed the ftudy of eloquence,
which afterwards became the firft ambition of the young nobility.

The Roman Hiftory informs us what
kind of citizens thefe men were who were
thus educated; they degenerated by degrees, and left a ftanding leffon to after-
times, of the confequences of preferring

learning

learning to virtue, and politenefs to mo-
rality.

From this brief review of ancient education and manners, it appears, what
were the opinions of the ancients. That
all wife and well regulated ftates, underftood that nature had need to be inftructed
by cultivation, and rectified by difcipline; and that they agreed in bringing
them up in ftrict fubjection to their parents and teachers.

We may obferve likewife, that a relaxation in education and difcipline leads
to a general corruption of manners.

———

Here ends my firft Effay upon this fubject; it is an introduction to what follows;
if it fhould be tedious to your ladyfhip,
I can abridge the reft, but I wifh you to
read the fubftance of them before you
come to my Plans, for they are founded

upon

upon my reafonings and comparing that of others, and drawing inferences from the whole.

I am, Madam,

Your obliged and obedient fervant,

FRANCES DARNFORD.

LETTER

LETTER V.

MRS. DARNFORD TO LADY A——.

HAVING learned the opinions of the ancients, let us briefly review thofe of the moderns, with the advantages of the examples and warnings, arifing from the virtues and errors of thofe who went before them.

It feems that they have altered and re-fined their methods of education, but it does not appear that they have im-proved them.

Inftead of following the good and re-jecting the evil, they have fallen into dif-putes concerning both ; rather chufing to fhew their fkill in wrangling and difputa-tion, than feeking the benefit of mankind ; and fhewing their vanity rather than their wifdom. In the mean time they have

gradually

gradually relaxed in all kinds of difcipline ; and no where more than in this country.

Since the difciplinarian method has been exploded, we have gone by rapid fteps to the other extreme, and become advocates for all kinds of relaxation. — In Milton's time, his fyftem of education might have been practicable, but in our days, men are not virtuous enough to follow it.

Locke's Syftem of Education was admired by all wife and virtuous parents : it was admired but not followed. Madame de Genlis has accounted for this with her ufual penetration and fagacity :

" Locke's work was tranflated into all " languages. It was in every body's " hand's when Rouffeau's Emilius ap- " peared;—but had not brought about " any change in the fyftems adopted. " Wifdom has lefs influence than enthu-
" fiafm,

" fiafm, becaufe it is always fimple in its
" expreffions, and fcarce ever affumes an
" impofing or authoritative tone.—The
" Englifh philofopher only feemed to
" give his advice ; Rouffeau repeated the
" fame things, but he did not advife ; he
" commanded, and was obeyed."

She likewife obferves, that Rouffeau follows the fyftem of Mr. Locke in almoft every refpect ; he copies him literally, but without quoting him, or acknowledging his obligations to him. It is thus that many other French writers have imitated out beft authors on moft fubjects.

Rouffeau has done much harm by encouraging a general relaxation of difcipline, and he has uttered many falfe dogmas, that would have been laughed at from any other man ; particularly that *one man* can only educate *one pupil* ; which experience proves to be falfe and abfurd ; neverthelefs, in his writings are many
excellent

excellent and admirable things, and it is much to be wished that the grain could be separated from the chaff.

That children are to be restrained without cruelty, and instructed without severity, can never be too strongly inculcated. That there is no necessity of scourging them through a course of learning, which they cannot attain by a gentle and moderate course of instruction.

The points mistaken and too strongly urged, have seemed to countenance the opinions of those who oppose all manner of subjection; but the truth is, that people ought to study the capacities and dispositions of their children, not only before they destine them to any particular calling or profession, but before they resolve on the course of education they are to go through.

Those youths who cannot profit by a learned

learned education, may yet do fo by an ufeful one, and may be better members of the community, than thofe who fpend fo large a portion of their time in the ftudy of the dead languages, or in other kinds of learning, of more credit than utility.

But above all other kinds of learning, the firft principles of religion and virtue fhould be early fown and ftrongly inculcated, they are not to be left to their own vague opinions, but the great outlines are to be written upon their hearts in ftrong and indelible characters. Here we turn afide from the fceptical Rouffeau, and follow the inftructions of a greater mafter.

" Train up a child in the way he fhould go, and when he is old he will not depart from it.

" Precept muft be laid upon precept, and line upon line; here a little and there a little."

I fhall

I ſhall here conclude this letter, but ſhall ſoon ſend another; in the interim, I remain your ladyſhip's moſt humble ſervant,

FRANCES DARNFORD.

LETTER

LETTER VI.

MRS. DARNFORD TO LADY A———.

DEAR LADY A———,

WITH your permiffion I am going to devolve the honour of your daughter's education upon a perfon every way fo much my fuperior, that I am proud to be thought one the humbleft pupils of her fchool, from whom I have received much information, which I have modified and adapted to the ufe of thofe in whofe education I have been con-cerned.

This perfon is an excellent French lady, firft known to our country by the name of Madame de Genlis; next, that of the Countefs de Sillery; and, thirdly, Madame de ————. I prefume her works are already known to your ladyfhip. The Theatre of Education, and the Tales of

the

the Caftle, are calculated for childhood and youth ; Adelai and Theodore, or a Syftem of Education, is a *fchool for parents.*—I have heard this laft work much criticifed, and to my thinking, by people who ftood in moft need of its affiftance. They ftudied to find faults in it, but they were unfuccefsful, and only fhewed their malice or their bad tafte.

What they chiefly dwelt upon was, its being calculated only for people of high rank and fortune ; and not practicable for people in the middling and lower claffes of life.—My anfwer was nearly as follows.—I cannot fuppofe it was ever defigned to be ftrictly and literally followed, but every degree in life may extract from it fuch things as are ufeful and practicable for themfelves ; and it is the peculiar excellency of this book, that every perfon may have recourfe to it, and find whatever is neceffary for their circumftances. There was

but

but little faid, in reply to my eulogium,
but difdainful and farcaftic looks fupplied
the place of argument. I wondered at
firft what could have given offence, but
upon further reflection, I perceived the
reafon. Parents do not like to be fent to
fchool; nor to be fhewn the defects of their
own education, nor of that they intend for
their children.

I have fuch entire confidence in the
lady to whom I have the honour to write,
that I believe fhe is willing to hear the
words of truth, ready to embrace its direction, and to fulfil all the duties that fhe
has undertaken, therefore I fpeak to her
without referve. There is no education
for daughters equal to that which they receive under the eye of a good mother,
who herfelf gives, or fuperintends it, according to her degree and fituation. But
it is not incumbent on your ladyfhip to
go and fhut yourfelf up in an old caftle in

Wales,

Wales, or the Highlands, in order to educate your daughters. You have other duties to fulfil, and an eminent degree to dignify.

You may fet apart a place for the purpofe of the young ladies and their governefs; for I difapprove much bringing them forward too foon, and introducing them into all company. Madame D'Almane carried her children from Paris, left they fhould be infected with the contagion of fafhionable manners, before their reafon, ftrengthened by good principles, fhould be ftrong enough to refift them, and to defpife them. In this point we may and ought to imitate her. Is not fafhion become the arbiter of manners in our own country?—or is fhe not rather a tyrant, who impofes laws, which we defpife and proteft againft, even in the moment that we fubmit to them? It is referved for a future generation, to withftand and

to deftroy her influence; and we take fome
fteps towards it, when we give our children an education which will enable
them to refift and defpife her abfurd dic-
tates.

To their own apartment I would confine my pupils, but not as prifoners; they
fhould fee and converfe with their mother
as often as her leifure or inclination leads
her to them; and they fhould fee her
chofen friends.

I would not chufe for them a governefs
with a countenance as harfh and forbidding as that of the Emperor Vefpafian;
the eye requires to be pleafed, before the
Judgment is exercifed.

I do not mean that the governefs fhould
be handfome; but only that fhe fhould
not be difgufting or forbidding in her af-
pect. She fhould certainly be mild and
amiable in her temper and manners, fhe is
to be their friend, their companion, and
                                    fometimes

fometimes their play-fellow; fhe fhould take a fhare in their paftimes, fhould fing and dance with them; in fhort, fhe fhould conciliate their regards; and their obedience fhould be that of love. I do not conceive that Adelaide could love Mifs Brigdet, though fhe might refpect her as her governefs.

I difapprove extremely the falfe confidence made to Adelaide, in order to teach her to keep a fecret:—it muft leffen Mifs Bridget in her efteem, and her confidence in her in future. Falfehood fhould never be fhewn, but to be punifhed; truth is the foundation of all moral virtue; and where it is wanting, or doubtful, we can have no reliance upon any perfon whatever. I think this the moft exceptionable of any thing in this fyftem of education; and I believe your ladyfhip will be of my opinion.

We will not fend our pupils to Laga-

D raye,

raye, we can fhew them many Lagaraye's in England, of which I fhall fpeak further hereafter : neither will we go to Bröeck to fee the happy peafants there. You have fhewn them Naples and its charming environs ; they have obferved the manners of different countries ; but they fhould ftill travel by the book, and read the lateft accounts of all the countries in the world ; the bleffing of Providence to every one peculiarly, fhould be pointed out to them, and they fhould be taught to love God, as the Father of *all his creatures*.

With all thefe abatements, which are only the marks of imperfection, which will adhere to all mortal fabrications, the fyftem of Madame de Genlis feems to me the moft perfect of any ; and it may certainly be followed fafely by fuch parents as are defirous of inftilling right principles into the hearts of their children; and who refolve to educate their minds in

preference

preference to their bodies, which may be done without neglecting any real accomplishment to the latter.

Though there is much to be disapproved in Rousseau's system, there is also much to be approved, and some things to be admired.

A wise parent and preceptor will extract from it what is useful and practicable; as the bee sucks honey from various flowers, and leaves the noxious qualities behind.

Thus, though we would not neglect sowing the first seeds of virtue, or of knowledge, till a child should ask for them; yet we should be very careful not to over-load the tender mind too early, nor to oppress it with such things as are above its comprehension. Rousseau would not exercise children's memories, in getting by heart any thing by way of task. I think with him, that this is frequently

carried too far to gratify the vanity of the
parent or preceptor, who are flattered by
the fuppofed prematurity of the child's
underftanding. But furely the memory
may be employed, without being oppref-
fed; and memory, like all other talents,
is improved and encreafed by exercife.—
If the child took pleafure in it, I would
encourage it with the utmoft caution, to
direct it properly that it might lay in a
ftore of fuch things as would be ufeful
hereafter. Some teachers except to their
getting any thing in poetry, but confine
them wholly to profe. I fee no reafon for
this; I think that the rhyme is more likely
to fix it in the memory, and that it retains
better what is got by heart in this way.
In this I fpeak from experience. I learned
many things, very early, in poetry, and
they are written upon my memory with a
pen of adamant, and nothing can erafe
them.

They

They were chiefly from Gay's Fables — Cotton's Visions—Parnel's Hermit—and extracts from our best poets.

I have much more to say upon these subjects, but I shall wait to hear from your ladyship; you must tell me truly whether I must transcribe all that I have written in this way, or whether I must abridge in future. When I have finished my Remarks, I shall come to the Plans themselves.

I am always, my dear Lady,

Your faithful and obedient servant,

FRANCES DARNFORD.

LETTER

LETTER VII.

LADY A———, TO MRS. DARNFORD.

I OWE my dear Mrs. Darnford more than I can ever repay, for her generous endeavours to be of service to me and my children. It is you that are the induftrious bee, collecting honey from various gardens, and offering to me the precious fruits of your labours, without any trouble on my part.

I receive this treafure with a due fenfe of its value, I intreat you to continue your communications, to abridge nothing, but to give me your thoughts at large, and what farther remarks may arife out of the fubjects before you. I have read the works of Madame de Genlis, but I fhall read them again with new and increafed relifh from your recommendation. I did not give them due confideration at

the

the time, but I fhall, at my next perufal, and, I doubt not with much advantage.

I thank you alfo for your Extracts, and your pupils for tranfcribing them; but I am almoft angry with Mrs. Stridtland, who directs them.—The Extracts are fo fhort *, that they want connection; and if I had not the higheft opinion of you, I fhould think you wifhed to conceal fome things from me. Why did you leave your hufband fo precipitately, after facrificing every thing to his deliverance? — You muft fupply thefe connecting parts to me either by letter, or by your prefence.— When do you come to town?—I will fee you there, be affured, and as often as I can.—In the mean time, continue your Remarks, and go through them.—I want

* This was owing to Mrs. Darnford's directions to her friend, to omit every thing relative to Lord A—'s behaviour, during her hufband's lifetime; and only o mention what was likely to do him credit with his lady.

to fee your Plans of Education, and, in
fhort, all your writings.

You mention my lord fo briefly, and run
away from him, that I fear you have not
heartily forgiven him. Let my friendfhip,
and his conduct in future, erafe all difagreeable recollections in relation to the paft,
and let the remainder of our lives be dedi-
cated to virtuous friendfhip.

I am yours, unfeignedly,

LOUISA A———.

LETTER

LETTER VIII.

MRS. DARNFORD TO LADY A———.

DEAR LADY A———,

I AM highly gratified by your approbation of my Remarks, and fomewhat concerned that you are not fatisfied with my Extracts; I take whatever blame is incurred, to myfelf; when we meet, I will fill up the deficiencies for you; in the mean time I will proceed with my Remarks, fome of which were written many years ago, and others added at the inftant of tranfcribing.

I prefume to affirm, that there has been a great alteration in the manners of this country, within the laft twenty or thirty years. More frequent inftances of atrocious crimes, murders, frauds, perjury; more frequent inftances of conjugal infidelity, and of divorces in confe-

quence;

quence; more people ruined by gam-
bling; obliged to fell the inheritance of
their fathers, and take fhelter in obfcurity;
more inftances of profligacy in manners;
and inftead of being afhamed of their
vices, men affume a boldnefs that fets all
order and decorum at defiance, and looks
virtue out of countenance.

When we reflect upon the manners of
the youth of our times, we cannot believe but there is fomething wrong in the
prefent fyftem of education. If our young
men are effeminate, diffolute, and impru-
dent; if our daughters are pert and ignorant, affected and diffipated, we may
draw thefe conclufions, in defiance of
Rouffeau and all his difciples—that fome
reftraint is abfolutely neceffary in the education of the youth of both fexes.

That a too early introduction into *life*,
as it is called, is deftructive of that fweet
modefty and delicacy, which was by na-

ture

ture intended for the guard of virtue;
that a too early and too frequent inter-
courfe between the fexes, deftroys the
purpofe it is intended to promote, and inftead of matrimony produces celibacy;
renders them cheap in the eyes of each
other, and upon further familiarity, there
grows more contempt, as Slender fays,
and as other obfervers can bear witnefs.

On the contrary, if we look back to any
period of time, when the fons of Britain
were hardy, manly, and virtuous, and her
daughters modeft, delicate, and chafte;
we cannot doubt that they were well educated and well principled.

The modern man of fafhion and tafte
may bolt his argument, and with a look
of defiance tell us—

" My grandmother told me, what her grandmother
told her," &c.

but we will anfwer, in the words of a
more refpectable writer :

D 6

" I hate,

" I hate when Vice can bolt her arguments,
" And Virtue has no tongue to check her pride ;
" For thou art worthy that thou ſhouldſt not know
" More happineſs than this thy preſent lot.—
" Enjoy your dear wit, and gay rhetoric ;
" Thou art not fit to hear thyſelf convinced.

MILTON'S COMUS.

All people of ſober minds are well convinced of this degeneracy of manners ;
and many writers of emiuence have endeavoured to ſtem the torrent of diſſipa-
tion ; and have given faithful warning of
the precipices, which men ſhut their eyes
to avoid ſeeing.

Every rank and degree of people, bring
up their children in a way above their ſituation and circumſtances ; they ſtep over
their proper place, and ſeat themſelves
upon a higher form.—They aſſume an air
of conſequence ; and the children of far-
mers, artificers and mechanics, all come
into the world as gentry. —They ſend
them to the ſame ſchools with the firſt
gentry in the county, and they fancy
themſelves

themfelves their equals. When the far-mer's daughter goes home to fpend her Chriftmas, fhe difplays her improvements and accomplifhments; her parents admire and are proud of her. Not fo the young lady; on her part, fhe difcovers that her papa and mama fpeak a very bad lan-guage; that their manners are unpolite; and, in fhort, that they are very vulgar people. In confequence of this difcovery fhe defpifes them, and their admonitions become a fubject of ridicule.—She turns her back upon them; fhe afpires to a genteel acquaintance, fhe catches the con-tagion of fafhion; and this finifhes her education.

What numbers of young ladies of this ftamp are turned into the world to feek their fortunes; boafting of their good education, ignorant of every thing ufeful, difdaining to match with their equals, afpir-ing to their fuperiors, with little or no

fortune,

fortune, unable or unwilling to work for themfelves.

Perhaps one in ten thoufand of thefe may make her fortune, all the reft conclude they fhall do the fame ; and thus they go on practifing the airs and graces of a fine lady till youth is paft, and then difcover, in after life, that they have been acting a part above them, without means to fupport it.

Unfortunate is the man who takes a wife out of this clafs of young ladies ; fhe will expect the fame luxuries and indulgencies as if fhe had brought him a plentiful fortune; but far the greater numbers of them become ufelefs, and fome, mifchievous members of fociety.

I would fimplify every mode of education, and render it eafy and practicable. —Every method fhould be adapted to the degree and fituation of the children it belongs to.

I would

I would inftitute feminaries of education for this purpofe; at leaft, I would point out, what might and what ought to be done, to make them anfwer the end propofed.

Perhaps your ladyfhip may fmile at fome of my Plans; perhaps you may think them only windmill fchemes.—Yet they may point out the way to others, who may hereafter improve upon my hints, and reduce them to practice. With this hope I tranfcribe and correct them, and perfuade myfelf that I am ufefully employed.

May I not hope that they will afford your ladyfhip amufement for a leifure hour, and a fubject for more ferious reflection afterwards?

I am, Madam,

Your moft obedient fervant,

F. DARNFORD.

LETTER

L E T T E R IX.

MRS. DARNFORD TO LADY A———.

I HAVE infifted on the gradations of rank and fortune being obferved in the education of children, in their drefs, manners, and introduction into life; but I am aware of the difficulty of reducing my doctrine, fo as to render it practicable.

But where fhall we draw the line that feparates the feveral orders and degrees of men, efpecially in a commercial ftate like this, and under a mixed form of government?

The nobility of this land are rich and powerful, but there is a diftinction between the different degrees and titles, and alfo between the old and new nobility, which the old families well underftand.

The next order, are the old families of wealth and confequence; fome of whom

have

have refufed titles that they thought it
beneath them to accept; whofe families
are older, and their fortunes fuperior to
many of the nobility.

In the third clafs, I would place thofe
who have acquired great wealth by any
profeffion or calling, and whofe wealth,
however gained, ftands in lieu of birth,
merit, and accomplifhments, to the world,
and alfo to themfelves. I mean only thofe
overgrown and enormous fortunes which
we have feen in our days; of which we
have feen the rife, progrefs, declenfion
and fall; which have mouldered away like
a rotten building, and have left nothing
but dirt and rubbifh behind.

Fourthly, I would reckon the inferior
gentry, who can only count hundreds,
where the above claffes number thoufands
a year. In this clafs every real bleffing
and comfort of life is to be found, and
thofe who know how to enjoy them, with
virtue

virtue and moderation, are the wifeft and happieft of mankind.—But there is a canker-worm which too frequently deftroys their fortunes and their happinefs; a foolifh ambition to imitate their fuperiors, in manners, in vanity, in expence. The influence of fafhion on the manners, like the fyftem of influence in government, pervades all orders and degrees of men.

The ftately Englifh oak is undermined by vile vermin who prey upon its roots; and while it looks fair to the eye for a while, it will fall before its decay is perceived.

" The oaks of Old England are wither'd away."

But, fifthly, the men of genteel profeffions, law, phyfic, and divinity; to thefe may be added, thofe employed in the public offices under government, and the officers of the army and navy. In this clafs I would include all merchants

of

of eminence. The character of a British merchant, is one of the most respectable of any in the world. Freed from narrow prejudices, by an intercourse with all nations, he acts upon a more enlarged scale; integrity, generosity, honour, and hospitality, are the pillars that support his character in all parts of the world.

" There, where his argosies with portly sail,
" Like seigniors and rich burghers of the flood,
" Or, as it were the pageants of the sea;
" Do overpeer the petty traffickers,
" That curtsie to them, do them reverence,
" As they fly by them with their woven wings."

SHAKESPEARE.

There are many of this honourable profession who can afford to spend with any of the classes abovementioned; but they are the best and wisest men, who provide for their families, and avoid all useless and impertinent display of their wealth. Since the increase of luxury and extravagance,

each

each of thefe orders are treading upon the
heels of the other—

    —" and even the toe of the peafant comes fo near
" the heel of the courtier, that he hurts his kibe."

SHAKESPEARE.

But let us go through with the gradation. The next, which I fhall call the fixth
order, will include all retail traders, artificers, and mechanics ; and the farmer
who rents his lands, and is a more ufeful
member of fociety than any of the reft ;—
he is likewife the moft refpectable, as
long as he keeps within his degree and
calling, but when he fteps over it, he
becomes ridiculous and contemptible in
the eyes of his fuperiors, and lays a
foundation of mifery and ruin for himfelf ;
if his houfe is as well-furnifhed as that of
his landlord; if he keeps as good a cellar
of wine ; and entertains his company with
the beft provifions of all kinds;—if his
wife and daughters are dreft in the fafhion;
if the young ladies, inftead of learning to

make

make butter and cheefe at home, are fent
to a boarding-fchool, are taught to dance,
to fpeak bad French, and to affume the
airs of town-bred ladies ; wretched is
the man who thus fools away his own advantages, and he will find his latter days
miferable, however profperous might be
the beginning ones. Can he wonder that
his landlord raifes his rent upon him?
He reafons fairly—if this man can live as
well as I do, in all refpects, why fhould
not I fhare his advantages ? Hence will
appear the folly of emulating our fuperiors, of imitating their manners; and
this reafoning will extend to every order
and degree, who over-leap the ftation they
belong to.

But let us take a brief review of the
the feventh clafs, which will include the
loweft mechanics and artizans, and the
whole peafantry of the land.—In this numerous and ufeful body of men, we muft
look

look for our foldiers and failors, fervants
and workmen of all and every kind;
thefe are the body of the people, thefe are
the ftrength and finews of the nation ; for
thefe, laws are framed, and properties fe-
cured. Every thing fhould be done for
their fupport and protection ; and every
check fhould be laid upon their attempts
to imitate the vanities and vices of the
higher orders, for even in the loweft ftations, they are not free from this predominant folly of the times. As the afs in
the fable, imitated the frifks and gambols
of the lap-dog, fo do thefe people the
fafhions and follies of their fuperiors.

The monfter, Fafhion, extends her influence to the whole circle, and the far-
theft round has its fhare of her fcepter of
rule. This is one part of the degeneracy
I complain of, and this, I hope, I have
brought fufficient proofs of.

Within every one of thefe orders of

men,

men, there is a gradation of property that raifes the firft ftep of it nearly to an equality with the next above it, and this increafes the difficulty of keeping them within their proper bounds.

In a well regulated ftate, a right and true fubordination is beautiful, where every order is kept in its proper ftate, and none is allowed to encroach upon, or opprefs another. But where is this ftate to be found ?—In Utopia, perhaps.

Let us then enquire where it is beft defcribed.—I will apply to a great mafter, in whom a ray of Divine wifdom, like that of his own Minerva, pointed out both to princes and people, their refpective duties and obligations :

" Pour le dedans de la Ville, Mentor vifita toutes
" les magafins, toutes les boutiques d'artizans, &
" toutes les marchandifes des pays etrangers qui
" pouvoient introduire le luxe et la moleffe.
" Il regla les *habits*, la nourriture, les meubles, les
" grandeurs, & l'ornement des maifons pour toutes les
" conditions differentes, il bannit tous les ornemens
" d'or

" d'or & d'argent; & il dit à Idomenée : je ne con-
" nois qu'un feul moyen pour rendre un peuple mo-
" defte dans fa dépenfe, c'eft que vous lui en donniez
" vous-meme l'exemple. Il eft neceffaire que vous
" ayez une certaine majefté dans votre extérieur, mais
" votre autorité fera affez marquée par vos gardes,
" & par les principaux officiers qui vous environnent.
" Contentez-vous d'une habit de laine tres-fine teinte
" en pourpre ; que les principaux de l'état aprés vous
" foient vetus de la meme laine ; & que toute la dif-
" ference ne confifte que dans la couleur, & dans une
" legere broderie d'or que vous aurez fur le bord de
" votre habit : ces differentes couleurs ferviront à
" diftinguer les differentes conditions, fans avoir be-
" foin ni d'or, ni d'argent, ni de pierreries. Reglez
" ces conditions par la naiffance, & mettez au premier
" rang ceux qui ont une nobleffe plus ancienne, &
" plus éclatante. Ceux qui auront le merite & l'au-
" torité des emplois, feront affez contens de venir
" aprés ces anciennes & illuftres familles, qui font
" dans une fi longue poffeffion des honneurs. Les
" hommes qui n'ont pas la meme nobleffe, leur ce-
" deront fans peine, pourvu que vous ne les accou-
" tumiez pas à ne fe point méconnoitre dans une trop
" haute & trop prompte fortune, & que vous donniez
" des louanges à la moderation de ceux qui font mo-
" deftes dans la profperité. La diftinction la moins ex-
" pofée à l'envie eft celle qui vient d'une longue fuite
" d'ancetres. Pour la vertu elle çera aprés excitée,
" & l'on aura affez d'empreffement à fervir l'état,
" pourveu que vous donniez des couronnes & des
" ftatues aux belles actions, & que ce foit un com-
" mencement de nobleffe pour les enfans de cieux
" qui les auront faites. Les perfonnes du premier

" rang

" rang après vous feront vetues de blanc avec une
" frange d'or & d'argent au bas de leur habit: ils
" auront au doigt un anneau d'or. Ceux du fecond
" rang feront vetus de bleu, ils porteront une frange
" d'argent avec l'anneau & point de medaille.—
" Les troifiémes de verd & fans frange, mais avec
" la medaille.—Les quatriémes d'un jaune d'aurore.
" —Les cinquiémes d'un rouge pale ou de rofes.—
" Les fixiémes de gridelin.—Les feptiémes qui feront
" les derniers du peuple d'une couleur melée de
" jaune & de blanc. Voilà les habits de fept condi-
" tions differentes pour les hommes libres; les ef-
" claves feront habillez de gris brun. Ainfi fans
" aucune dépenfe, chacun fera diftingué fuivant fa
" condition, & on bannira de Salente tous les arts qui
" ne fervent qu'à entretenir le fafte. Tous les arti-
" zans qui feront employez à ces arts pernicieux
" s'uniront ou aux arts neceffaires qui font un petit
" nombre, ou au commerce, ou à l'agriculture. On
" ne fouffrira jamais aucun changement ni pour la na-
" ture des étofes, ni pour laforme dés habits; car il eft
" honteux que des hommes deftinez à une vie ferieufe
" & noble s'amufent à inventer des parures affectées,
" ni qu'ils permettent que leurs femmes, à qui ces
" amufemens feroient moins honteux tombent iamais
" dans cet excez."

TELEMAQUE, Livre 12ieme.

Oh, that kings, princes, and legifla-
tors, would ftudy Telemachus!—That
they would become the fhepherds of
their people !—That they would protect

E   and

and provide for them ; and not join with the wolves who lie in wait to prey upon them, upon condition that they fhould enjoy the largeft fhare of their fleeces, and enrich themfelves with their fpoils !

Forgive me this apoftrophe, fuggefted by the divine Fenelon ! —whofe virtues were his crimes, under the reign of Louis XIV. who never forgave thofe lef-fons which expofed the defects of his go-vernment, and taught his grandfon how to correct them, if he had lived to fucceed to the throne.

The revival of fumptuary laws is de-voutly to be wifhed, but not greatly to be hoped for; I acknowledge that many dif-ficulties lie in the way, and that there would be no immediate advantages to in-duce government to undertake it ; there could no greater motive be propofed than the good of the people.

I have been confidering, whether any
                                        kingdom

kingdom in Europe has attempted to introduce them; I think there is a regulation of this kind in Sweden, but I am not quite certain of it.

There is not much greater reason to expect a reformation of this kind, from convincing people of the fitnefs and propriety of it;—perhaps a good and virtuous education would go further than any other method : by teaching youth to afpire to fuperior qualities, they might be taught to defpife the paltry diftinctions of drefs and fafhion.

I will relieve your ladyfhip from this fubject, by affuring you of my unfeigned efteem and refpect at all times—to which I will fign my hand and heart,

FRANCES DARNFORD.

LETTER

LETTER X.

MRS. DARNFORD TO LADY A——.

MY DEAR LADY,

I WILL fuppofe that you have reco-
vered from the fatigue of my late in-
veftigation, and are prepared to go on with
me in my progrefs through the reft of my
fubject.

I have led you from the top of a high
hill, down into a fpacious valley, from
whence we can fall no lower. The rich
and the proud look down with difdain
from their high habitations, but we will
not doubt to find many beautiful flowers,
fruits, and herbs ; we fhall alfo find many
noxious weeds, which we will endeavour
to eradicate, that the herbs of value may
thrive the better.

Fenelon divides his nation into feven
orders of men ; after which he fpeaks of

an

an eighth, which he calls flaves. Whom does he mean, think you?—Surely, not the peafantry; they ought not to be flaves; they are not fo with us; but I fear, in his time, they were little lefs in France; and he could not forefee that a time fhould come, when they fhould be delivered from the yoké of tyranny, and become freemen.

There have been in all times and all countries a fet of men in the moft abject ftate of fervitude, and it refted with their mafters to render their fituation tolerable or miferable. In fome countries they made the captives they took in war perform their moft fervile offices. The Spartans kept a whole diftrict in this ftate of flavery, to do fuch offices as they held too mean for the citizens of Sparta.—I fpeak of the Helotes, whofe treatment was at leaft as bad as the negroes receive from their mafters in the fugar iflands.

E 3   The

The Romans treated their flaves more
liberally; they diftinguifhed thofe of fuperior merit from the herd of men. They
gave to young men of talents the beft
education; they raifed them to offices of
truft, and fometimes made them their
companions.

They were frequently freed entirely
from fervitude; and the number of freed-
men, became almoft equal to the de-
nizens.

In the Hiftory of the Jews, we find
that a whole nation, or rather the inhabitants of a fmall diftrict, were condemned
to be hewers of wood and drawers of
water to the children of Ifrael.

There were alfo flaves of another kind
among the Jews, as houfehold fervants;
and they were enjoined to treat them with
humanity.

In all the Eaftern countries, it has always been common to have many flaves;

in

in all great cities they have flave markets, where both men and women are bought and fold like cattle, and how they fhall be treated, depends entirely upon the purchafers. Cervantes gives an account of their treatment in his admirable Don Quixotte ; and, under feigned names, relates the adventures of himfelf and his companions during their flavery at Algiers, particularly in the charming ftory of the Captive.

In Spain and Italy there are focieties of charitable perfons, for the redeeming of Chriftian captives in Turky and other Mahometan countries ; this charity reflects honour upon its donors.

If thoufands of Europeans are in actual flavery, and tens of thoufands in a ftate of oppreffion, does it not feem a ftrange kind of Quixottifm, to demand an abolition of the flave trade to Africa, and the emancipation of the negroes? There

are among us a fet of men who are engaged in this caufe, and who purfue it
with an ardour and perfeverance that
would do honour to a better; for furely
they have made choice of improper objects on which to exercife their charity.——
I have heard and read all the arguments
on both fides; and, upon a fair and im-
partial furvey and confideration, it appears to me, that if they could carry their
points, they would be injurious to the
commerce of this land, and no benefit
to the objects they wifh to relieve.

I have been affured, both by natives of
the Weft Indies, and by thofe occafionally
refident there, that the accounts given by
the patrons of the negroes are in fome inftances falfe, and in moft of the others
highly exaggerated. That they are, in general, much happier there than in their na-
tive country ; that the grief and fullennefs
they fhew, when they are firft carried over,

is ⸺

is owing to an apprehenfion that they are faved only to be killed and eaten; and that, when this is cured, they foon recover their health and fpirits ;—that they are lazy and obftinate beyond conception, and muft be governed by ftrict difcipline; that they are malicious and revengeful, and, if they had the power, would be cruel.

If their mafters were cruel enough to inflict ftripes and torments upon them, merely to gratify their humours, their intereft would forbid it; but it is to be hoped, this can fcarce ever happen.— Englifhmen were never reckoned cruel, though there may have been fome inftances of it, as there have of the moft exalted virtues in the negro race; but thefe do not characterize a whole nation. It is degrading our country and countrymen, to fuppofe them guilty of wanton cruelty to their flaves, and then to reafon upon it, as if it were generally true. Could our enemies fpeak worfe of us than our brethren have done?

If what the Weft Indians affert be true, that eveiy negro has a little fpot of ground, and is allowed time to cultivate it; that from thefe the markets are fupplied with vegetables; that from the produce of thefe, they are allowed to have merry meetings of their own race, with mufic, dancing, and other recreations; — that thofe who are careful and prudent frequently fave money enough to purchafe their freedom; if thefe things be true, and they have not been yet difproved, furely it would be better if the gentlemen engaged in the negro caufe would turn the current of their charity into another channel, and leave this matter as they found it.

That "Charity begins at home," is a proverb too often abufed by felfifh and

avaricious

avaricious people to cover their fordid difpofitions; but, in the cafe before us, it will
bear a more generous application. I will,
under fhelter of this proverb, prefume to
point out fome objects of Charity at
home, that claim attention from the public in general, and every generous and
worthy mind.

The firft objects I would bring before
them, fhould be *poor children* of all de-
nominations. Poor children put out to
parifh nurfes; poor children apprenticed
by the parifh, to people but one degree
lefs paupers than themfelves; to chimney-
fweepers, to bafket-makers, to fpinners,
throwfters, weavers, &c. &c.

Let a Committee of Enquiry be appointed from the charitable fociety, who
have taken the African negroes under their
protection. Let them enquire how thefe
poor children are treated; how they are
cloathed and fed: let them direct how

E 6   they

they fhall be brought up, fo as to become ufeful members of the community, and put out properly and likely to produce this effect. Let them inftitute fchools of induftry, to promote a reformation of manners of the lower orders of men; which are of as much importance as the manners of the great.

In all cities and great towns, there are numbers of poor children walking about half naked, hungry and wretched, without any vifible means of fupport. Thofe who can regard human nature, under this humiliating appearance, have followed them into lanes and allies, in the outfkirts of the towns, into miferable hovels and cottages, that could hardly keep out the wind and rain. Their parents without any trade or calling for the moft part :— they do not care to confefs how they live, nor what they defign for their children;

dren; but, moft probably, they are def-
tined to beggary or ftealing, perhaps
both. Human nature here is degraded to
its loweft ftate, even below flavery. I will
fuppofe the Committee abovementioned
to pick up thefe wretched creatures; to
purchafe fome old houfe, run to ruin,
for them to repair and make it habitable,
and to found a fchool of induftry. I
would clothe them in the moft ordinary
materials, if it were in coarfe canvas, it
would be better than rags and filthinefs.
They fhould wear wooden fhoes, not fuch
as the peafants wear in France, but fuch
as I have feen made for the prifoners in the
lately erected gaol for the county of Suf-
folk. The upper part is of a thick,
ftrong leather, the fole is like the board of
a wooden clog or patten, and the upper
part is nailed all round. I have wifhed to
found a trade for this article, and to fend
them

them to all the bare-footed children
which I have met in my walks in the
outſkirts of a certain town. I would have
theſe children brought up to hard labour,
and qualified to get an honeſt livelihood.
They ſhould cultivate a piece of ground,
to provide them with vegetables of every
kind, which might produce the chief part
of their food.

As the youths grew up, and they had
ſtrength ſufficient, they might aſſiſt as
porters at wharfs and quays, or help ſaw-
yers and fellers of timber and other
works. In harveſt time, they ſhould
be let to work in the fields, at ſmall
prices ; and by the time they grew to
manhood, they might be able to earn an
honeſt living.

Behold my firſt and loweſt Plan of
Education !—which I dedicate with unfeigned reſpect to thoſe gentlemen, who
have

have taken the negroes under their protection. I perceive and admire their generous intentions ; and have no doubt that
they are at leaft equally ready to affift their
own countrymen, who claim and deferve
their notice, and folicit their charity.

I fhould add, that according to my
Plan, thefe paupers are not to be taught
to write or read ; being refcued from
extreme poverty, they are to be hewers
of wood and drawers of water, and to be
thankful for their deliverance ; but they
are to be taught their duties to God,
their neighbours, and themfelves ; and
to attend the fervice of the church regularly, and to ufe private devotions every
morning and evening ; and to know that
no undertaking can fucceed without the
bleffing of Heaven. When they enter
into life and can maintain themfelves, they
fhould be enjoined to contribute their
mite, though ever fo little, to the fupport
of

of their brethren, whom they leave in the fituation they have juft quitted.

Here I fhall conclude this letter, hoping to hear from your ladyfhip foon, with your remarks on my performance.

I am now, and at all times, your ladyfhip's obliged and obedient fervant,

FRANCES DARNFORD.

LETTER

LETTER XI.

LADY A—— TO MRS. DARNFORD.

DO not be angry with me, my dear Mrs. Darnford!—it is fo natural to communicate our pleafures to thofe we love beft, that I could not forbear fhewing your letters to Lord A——. He was fur-prifed to find you fo deep in knowledge of a national kind, and pleafed to fee you entering fo warmly into the beft interefts of mankind. He is pleafed that you have defended a due fubordination of rank, and that you do not wifh the boundaries thrown down, and all men put upon a level; becaufe he thinks, that in their dif-ferent degrees and occupations men are moft ufeful to each other, and that the refult is the harmony of the whole.

My lord fays, he can ftrengthen your

arguments

arguments againſt the emancipation of the
negroes, by two conſiderations; the firſt
is, the preſent conſequences; the ſecond,
the future. The firſt ſeems to be already
coming forward; namely, that the negroes,
being apprized of the ſteps that have been
taken here in their favour, are preparing to
riſe againſt their maſters, and to cut their
throats. We have heard of very late re-
bellions, that have, with difficulty, been
cruſhed, and we may expect to hear of
more daily.

The ſecond conſequence to be expected
is, that when the great point ſhall be carried for them, they will flock hither from
all parts, mix with the natives, and ſpoil
the breed of the common people. There
cannot be a greater degradation than this,
of which there are too many proofs already in many towns and villages.

The gradations from a negro to a white
are

are many : firſt, a black and a white produce a mulatto ; ſecondly, a mulatto with
a white produce a meſtee ; thirdly, a
meſtee and a white produce a quadroon,
a dark yellow ; the quadroon and a white,
a fallow kind of white, with the negro
ſhade, and ſometimes the features. All
theſe together produce a vile mongrel
race of people, ſuch as no friend to Britain can ever wiſh to inhabit it.

Theſe conſiderations ſhould be recommended to the patrons of the Black Bill
of Rights ; perhaps they may not have
reflected upon theſe points, and the miſchiefs they contain.

The king of the French, when he was
king of France, baniſhed all the negroes
from his country ; it would be wiſe to
do ſo in Britain, while it is yet in our
power.

You are to underſtand this reaſoning to
proceed

proceed from my lord ; who says farther, that he has no doubt to call the negroes an inferior race of men, but still a link of the universal chain, and, as men, entitled to humanity, to kindness, and to protection ; and he thinks, their masters ought to be amenable to the laws, if they overwork, or otherwise ill-treat them.

⊦ If we have known an Ignatius Sancho, and a Phillis Wheatly, they are exceptions to the general rules of judgment, and may be compared with a Bacon and a Milton, among the most civilised and refined of the race of Europeans.

Thus much is for my lord, and as a return for your thoughts, which you have communicated to us. For myself, I have travelled with you through all your gradations to the bottom of the valley ; and shall be happy to climb up again with you ; for I perceive you mean to ascend by the same gradation, and to give us your

Plan

Plan of Education for each, as you go along.

In the mean time, I want a governefs for my two girls; I wifh you could recommend one. They have with them at prefent a very good girl, rather above a fervant, and yet below a governefs; but I want a gentlewoman, better educated, upon whom I can occafionally devolve my authority. I expect to be confined for a month in the courfe of the winter; and I wifh for fuch a fubftitute as I have defcribed. I think, with you, that fhe fhould not have fo harfh a countenance as old Vefpafian, yet I had rather fhe was plain than handfome; I beg you to look out for fuch an one, and I fhall be ready to receive her as foon as fhe can come to me. My daughters underftand more Italian than they do French; I want a perfon completely miftrefs of the latter, and able to converfe with them in it daily.

I am

I am now reading Adelaide and Theodore, as it ought to be read; which, I
confefs, I did not before; I difcover a
thoufand beauties which l had overlooked,
or but flightly obferved. I afpire to imitate Madame d'Almane, wherever fhe is
imitable; there are fome parts of her character that are above my reach, and out
of my power. I honour and revere the
author of this book.

Your extract from Telemachus is very
fine and very wife, but I fear it is not re-
ducible to practice.

It is true that the influence of fafhion
has increafed and is increafing; infomuch,
that it is impoffible to guefs at people's
degree, by their appearance; with you I
fee it, but I do not fee how it can be re-
medied or prevented. People of fuperior rank and fortunes ufed to have the
privilege of enjoying their own vanities
and follies exclufively; but now they are
                                    imitated

imitated by the lower degrees, and nothing but abſolute poverty excludes them. This is a great evil, and there are many who offer up their comforts and conveniences at the ſhrine of the idol Faſhion.

I long to ſee the reſt of your Plans ; I have no doubt of their virtue and benevolence, I only wiſh they may be practicable. In impatient expectation of your next packet,

I am, dear Madam,

Your obliged and affectionate friend,

LOUISA A——.

LETTER

LETTER XII.

MRS. DARNFORD TO LADY A———.

INDEED, Madam, I owe you no thanks
for fhewing my letters to my Lord
A———. You expect me to be fincere ; I
did not intend them for his infpection :
but his remarks are very juft, and his arguments ftrengthen mine ; I am obliged
by his communications, though I had
rather not have given caufe for them.——
I have promifed to fend you my Plans
and my Remarks on Education and Manners ; I will not break my word with you,
but will continue to tranfcribe the papers
that lie before me.

The next degree I fhall fpeak to, are
the lower kinds of artizans and mechanics, fuch as are juft above want. Many
of thefe (I fear I may fay moft of them)

let

let their children run wild, and they are brought up in the ſtreets.—I uſed to walk upon an old rampart near the town where I lived ſome years ; it was always full of children decently clothed, and looking well fed, but wild as ſavages ; and I have heard from their mouths horrible oaths and curſes. Whenever they were rebuked and adviſed, they ſet up ſuch yells and ſhrieks, that I could have thought myſelf among the wild Indians in America, rather than in the midſt of England ; ſo rude and uncivilſed were theſe unhappy children. — This was their reſort, and ſuch were their daily practices; employment they had none ; they might have anſwered with Orlando —" I am taught to make nothing,"—to the enquirer : and, to their parents,—" We are helping you to mar that which God made; theſe poor unhappy children of yours with idleneſs." I once ſaw a woman correcting one of theſe, and driving him home to

F   dinner.

dinner. I expoſtulated with her. " How
can you expect your children to be
good and obedient, when they are
brought up in the high road, idle and
diſſolute, and converſe only with ſavages ?"   " Lack-a-day, Madam !" ſaid
ſhe, " I cannot help it.—I have enough
to do at home, and am glad to get rid of
my great boys a few hours in the day."
" So you turn them looſe upon the public, to get rid of the trouble of their company.—What ſort of men think you they
will make ?"   " How ſhould I know
that ?" ſaid ſhe.   " Suppoſing they ſhould
take bad courſes, as they are taught
no good ones ; ſuppoſing they ſhould
commit attrocious crimes, and come at
laſt to the gallows; will not you have reaſon to accuſe yourſelf, for being in no
ſmall degree the cauſe of it ?"   I don't
know, indeed; but if it ſhould be ſo,
'tis no buſineſs of yours."   " Yes it is,
if what I ſay tends to prevent it."   Here
ſhe

ſhe began to abuſe me, and I made haſte to get out of hearing, and made the beſt of my way home.

In villages, theſe things are leſs frequent; children are brought up more in the paths of nature and ſimplicity. In every pariſh there is at leaſt a dame's ſchool, and in large one's there is a reading and writing maſter; ſo that children are kept in order, and are taught the difference between good and evil; and on Sundays they are taught their duties at the pariſh church..

As to Sunday Schools, I have no great expectations from them; but they are popular, and it is thought a kind of hereſy to ſpeak againſt them.—It is Schools of *Induſtry* that are wanted, to reform the manners of the common people; where they are taught their duties *every day*, and *all the day long*. That theſe are practicable I can bring ſufficient proofs.

In

In the town of Shrewfbury, there is an
eftablifhment admirably conducted; which
not only fupports itfelf, but alfo provides
for its children; of this, I hope to obtain
further particulars.

I am informed that they are in print,
and therefore refer you to a pamphlet entitled, " Some Account of the HOUSE of
INDUSTRY at SHREWSBURY, its Eftablifhment, and Regulations; with Hints to
thofe who may have fimilar Inftitutions in
View.   By J. WOOD."

I am told there is a fecond edition of
this work, with confiderable additions,
by-laws, rules, and ordinances.

I know not why we may not fpeak of
living worthies, who do honour to their
times and countries, and fhow bright examples of benevolence to others, and who
ought to be recorded among the benefactors of mankind.   Mrs. Trimmer is one
of thofe, who, by her writings, and by
                                   her

her conduct, has contributed greatly to the reformation of the manners among the lower orders of people. She has inftituted fchools of induftry, and prefides herfelf over one of them ; her daughters affift her in this honourable employment, and it is a fight that angels might behold with pleafure.

" Give her of the fruit of her hands, and let her works praife her."

PROVERBS OF SOLOMON.

There is a lady living in a certain great town in Effex, who has inftituted a fchool under her own eye, and given up the beft rooom in her houfe to this purpofe; where fifty poor children are clothed and educated in all the duties of their ftation. I do not prefume to name her, for fhe is one of thofe who

" Do good by ftealth, and blufh to find it fame."

POPE.

There are fome ladies of high rank,

F 3 who

who devote their time and abilities to the good of mankind ; and. feem to attone for the extravagance and diffipation of others.

There are among us, gentlemen, who fet apart a portion of their annual revenue to this noble and generous purpofe.

I have faid that there are many Lagaraye's in England, and I hope I have brought fufficient proofs of it. But every one cannot do thefe things, they are only for people of large fortunes. Very true ; but every one can contribute according to their ability, and fome plan might be laid down, wherein every ones mite would be of fervice. For inftance :

A PLAN FOR
A SCHOOL OF INDUSTRY
IN EVERY PARISH.

I would firft eftablifh in every parifh, a
Committee

Committee of Enquiry, such as I have
before mentioned ; it should confist of se-
ven perfons, of refpectable characters and
of known property. The chairman should
be the principal gentleman in the parish ;
or, if he diclined it, the next in fortune
and confequence. They should meet once
a week, to confult on means and meafures
for the well-governing the foeiety to be
formed. I fuppofe the Rector or Vicar
of the parish (if refident) to be always a
member of the fociety ; if he does not re-
fide, then the refident Curate.

The firft object of enquiry should be,
what fums of money are raifed in the parish for the relief of the poor, and how
they are employed. The fecond, to feparate the children and thofe able to work
from the fick and aged ; to the latter, the
greateft attention and tendernefs should be
paid ; and the former should be obliged
to work for their living.

From

From the beſt information I can procure, it does not appear that the preſent
Houſes of Induſtry have anſwered the expectations of the public. Many of them
are in debt, and ſome are not able to ſup-
port themſelves. I propoſe that mine
ſhall (after two or three years) maintain
themſelves at leaſt; and, in due time,
provide for the children.

In every one of theſe ſchools, a branch
of ſome kind of manufactory ſhould be
carried on. For inſtance: in one, weaving coarſe ſtuffs for clothing the poor;
this ſhould include all the different parts
of this buſineſs; carding the wool, ſpinning it, warping and winding, weaving
and dreſſing the ſtuffs, and they ſhould
have a ſhop, where they ſhould be ſold
for the benefit of the ſociety. In another,
ſpinning flax or hemp, preparing and
weaving coarſe linen, bleaching and dreſſing it, and afterwards ſelling it as abovementioned.

mentioned. In another, making facking and hop-bagging. In another, ftocking-weaving and hofiery. In another, carpenters and joiners work, turnery, &c.

In every one of thefe fchools, I would have a taylor and fhoemaker; and every thing made for the ufe of the fociety within itfelf.

Thefe trades fhould be well confidered by the Committe, before they are fet on foot; and it fhould be fo contrived, that two of the fame craft fhould not be placed too near each other; but every parifh a different trade for many miles round, and thus they would affift and promote each others intereft and advantage.

There are to be found in every place, young men who have ferved their apprenticefhip to a trade, and without means to fet up for themfelves; thefe might be engaged to the fociety for a term of years; at the end

F 5 of

of which (having ſerved it faithfully)
they ſhould be enabled, by the ſociety, to
go into buſineſs for themſelves, with the
additional advantage of a certificate of
recommendation, ſigned by at leaſt three
of the committee.

Suppoſing this to be practicable the advantages would be obvious. The poor's
rates would be reduced, the ſick and aged
properly attended, and they only taken
into the poor's houſe. The lazy would
be obliged to work, and they would be
induced to do it for themſelves, rather
than be obliged to work for others ; thus
many who throw themſelves and their families upon the pariſh, would maintain
them at home ; for lazy perſons are always ſelfiſh, and this quality would be
engaged on the behalf of induſtry.

I truſt there are in every pariſh, a ſufficient number of virtuous and benevolent
perſons, who would voluntarily take the
trouble

trouble of putting such plans as these into execution; the men would be committee men, the women patronesses of the societies.

The care of the parishes, would be taken out of the hands of crafty and designing people, who too often abuse their trust, and placed in the care of honest and responsible men, who would find themselves rewarded sufficiently in the love and confidence of their fellow-citizens, and the consciousness of being benefactors to the community. The committees might extend their enquiries still further, to the endowments and donations of their respective parishes, and the right application of them, to removing itinerant beggars, which are a nuisance in every parish. I only point out these to your consideration, but I have a great inclination to tell you a true story:

The

The bailiff or over-looker of a large farm in Effex, and a common beggar, were driven together by a thunder ftorm, and took fhelter at an ale-houfe. It was in the evening, and the landlord perfuaded them to fit down to fupper with him; each of them called for his pint of ale, and they converfed together as fellow-creatures, who were paffengers on the fame journey. After fupper the beggar-man faid to the bailiff, " Fellow-traveller, will you go fhares with me in a pint of punch?"—" No," faid the other, " I cannot afford it; a pint of ale is all my allowance."—" Then," faid the beggar, " your trade is not fo good as mine."— " Perhaps fo, but I think it is more honeft and more refpected."—" You prate of honefty; but you take what is given you as well as I."—" Yes, but I earn it firft by my fervices."—" Earn it; fo do I, and fometimes hardly enough. I can

beg

beg through three parifhes in a day, and
'tis a poor parifh that will not yield me
half-a-crown : it cofts me nothing for
lodging, except of a wet night. I always
have a good fupper and a tiff of punch
after it."—" Much good may it do you ;
but I will not change trades with you. I
have a quiet, happy home to go to,
where a good woman will give me a
chearful welcome. I maintain my family,
pay all my debts and dues, and can fhew
my face any where. You are a wanderer,
and a vagabond, that eat the bread that
fhould be for the poor labourer, and in-
tercept the charity that fhould be for the
fick and the needy ; and befide this, you
are liable to be taken up and punifhed for
thefe practices. No, I will not change
places with you on any terms ; we have
eaten together, and I will not betray you
into the hands of juftice ; but I will not
be your friend nor companion, but on
fuch

fuch an occafion as the prefent one."—
Choofe proud fool ! Go hug your chain,
fawn upon your mafter, who eats the
grain and gives you the chaff. I live the
life of a gentleman ; you, that of a dog."
—" Good words, Mr. Vagabond ! I don't
mean to quarrel with you, I refpect myfelf too much to dirty my hands upon you.
Farewel ; and may you meet with your
deferts !"—" Good b'ye, Iffachar ! Fare-
well, beaft of burthen !"—They feparated,
and each returned to his calling; and here
I will end my letter.

F. DARNFORD.

LETTER

LETTER XIII.

MRS. DARNFORD TO LADY A———.

WITH my dear Lady A———'s permiſſion, I will lay aſide ceremo-
ny, and proceed; aſcending the third ſtep
of my Plans.

I have ſaid already, that all kinds of
education ſhould be adapted to the ſituation of the pupils; I will add, and to
their future deſtination. In every town
you go through, you may ſee written in
letters of gold, " A Boarding School for
Young Ladies;" but did you ever ſee
one for thoſe that are not to act the parts
of young ladies? I believe not; they are
rarely to be found. All degrees are
blended together in theſe ſchools, to the
mutual diſadvantage of all the parties con-
cerned.

I have

I have no opinion of boarding fchools in general. I know that there are fome that fulfil every duty, and anfwer every purpofe of neceffary education ; but there is no kind of fchool equal to that inftruction which children receive at home, under a virtuous and well-informed mother, who gives up her time and abilities to the care of them. In truth, if all mothers fulfilled their duties, there would be little occafion for boarding-fchools ; but if they give up their time and attention to drefs, to vifiting, to cards, and to public places; it is better that the children fhould go to fchool, than that they fhould converfe with the fervants, or play in the ftreets.—There is a kind of mifcellaneous education among the lower kinds of gentry and tradefmen, which follows no particular fyftem, but is as good as the beft ; where the parents teach them their refpective duties and obligations, and leave it to

nature

nature to do the reft. This produces the
moft original characters, and fhews what
nature intended them. Education too,
merely confined to rules, produces " very
fine pictures, and all alike;" as Lady
Pentweafle fays; but fuch as I have laft
defcribed, retain the markings of nature.
—I have been furprifed at the variety of
characters in one family; and I have always imputed it to this caufe :—the early
part of education depends on the mother;
and men that are wife, will confider this in
the choice of their wives; for on them
they muft depend for the education and
principles of their chilren.

Serinda was left young a widow, with
a large family. She has educated fix
daughters, in the ftricteft principles of piety
and virtue; at the fame time, fhe has
given them every advantage in her power
in regard to ornamental accomplifhments.
They were educated in her own houfe, in
a country

a country village; fhe taught them the focial and relative duties, and enforced them by her own example. Her cares and attention have been well repaid, by the affection and confidence of her children, and by their happy eftablifhment under her maternal eye. They were early fought in marriage by fuch young men as wifhed for amiable companions, and faithful partners for life; five of them are married with the happieft profpects, and with their mother's entire approbation.

Charidema is a happy wife, and the mother of ten children; all educated under the eyes of their excellent parents, who have devoted themfelves to the moft ufeful of all employments, that of forming good and ufeful members of the community.

Their houfe is a feminary of education; the fons attend their father, and the daughters their mother, at the ftated

hours

hours of tuition; and even their amufe-
ments are fo directed, as to contribute to
their improveme: . The young people
do all the needle-work for the ufe of the
family; their mother and her fervants
fpin flax and hemp, at leifure hours,
fufficient to fupply the family with
houfehold linen. Decorum, prudence,
œcononny, and charity, prefide over this
well-governed family; and attract the efteem and veneration of all that approach
it.

It is with pleafure, with delight, that
amidft a too evident declenfion of manners, I can felect fuch examples, who do
honour to their country, and to human
nature. I am convinced, that fuch as thefe
poffefs all the real enjoyments of life, in
a much higher degree, than thofe who are
engaged in the purfuits of vanity, fafhion,
and diffipation. With thefe the duties of
a wife

a wife and mother are but lightly re-
garded; they transfer the care of their
children to governeſſes, or to ſervants;
they ſee them but ſeldom, and that merely
to ſatisfy their conſciences; in truth, the
children are no looſers in being ſeparated
from ſuch mothers. Where a mother is
unable, or unqualified to diſcharge the
duty of tuition herſelf; they are certainly
better placed in a good ſchool; as in the
caſe of Mrs. Ilford, with whom I lived a
few months. Too much care cannot be
taken in the choice of one, nor too cloſe
enquiry made into the conduct of it. I
have pointed out ſome of the evils and
miſchiefs that ariſe from young girls
being educated above their preſent
ſituation, and their future expectations in
life.

There are wanting among us ſchools of
a different kind, where young people
might

might acquire neceſſary and uſeful knowledge, without learning to ape the vanities and follies of their ſuperiors ; who, as your ladyſhip archly obſerves, uſed to have the privilege of enjoying them excluſively.

I never knew but one ſchool of this kind, and that ſunk when its founder and pillar was removed. A young woman of low birth and education, raiſed a ſchool in a country village, upon a very plain and ſimple plan ; ſhe had a good underſtanding and many uſeful qualifications.

She took twenty pupils; which were afterwards encreaſed to thirty. They aſſiſted her in doing the buſineſs of the houſe; they made the beds, and ſwept the rooms in turn ; after which, they ſat down to needlework of the moſt uſeful kinds. They were taught to read the Bible, and Common Prayer Book, in a plain, but not grammatical way. At

washing-

wafhing-times, they ftarched and ironed
the linen ; every one her own things.——
The miftrefs was elegantly neat in all her
doings, and properly qualified in all other
refpects to prefide over a fchool of this
kind.

This fchool flourifhed about ten years ;
when the miftrefs attracted the notice of
the 'Squire of the parifh, and her good
fortune fpoiled an excellent fchool-mif-
trefs, and made an awkward kind of a gentlewoman. She married the 'Squire, and
transferred the fchool to other hands, incapable of fupporting it ; and it funk,
never more to rife.

The new made lady, whom a book-
feller ufed to call, the Lady of the Laft
Edition, prefumed upon her merits ; took
upon her the ftile and dignity of a governefs, talked of books and of learning, as
if fhe really underftood them ; and by mif-
pronouncing half her words, and coining
others

others of no meaning at all, frequently raifed a fmile in the faces of thofe who knew her hiftory. A leffon to all thofe' who aim at a ftation above them, without the requifites to fupport it. In her fchool fhe was truly refpectable; and I wifh heartily I could fee more fuch fchools, and fuch women to govern them.

What I have faid, will apply to moft of thofe who are placed in the middle ftations of life, and who are apt to educate their children too highly for their deftination.

It is a melancholy confideration, to think of the numbers of young women who are turned loofe upon the world, over educated; without means to fupport themfelves, and difqualified to earn their living. There are very few trades for women; the men have ufurped two-thirds of thofe that ufed to belong to them; the remainder are over-ftocked, and there are

few

few refources for them. If they are handfome and amiable, their dangers are fo
much the more. Man who fhould be
their protector, turns their betrayer, and
too frequently abandons them to fhame
and poverty. How many are daily in danger of being ftarved. How many are condemned to menial fervices, for which their
enervated bodies and enfeebled minds,
render them wholly unqualified! Moft of
thefe are the victims of their parents pride
and vanity.

The falfe fentiments, falfe refinements,
and falfe fyftems of modern times, have
counteracted the laws of nature and reafon, and condemned a great number of women to a life of perpetual celibacy.

The adoration paid to wealth, the fuppo-
fititious wants which luxury impofes, have
induced many parents to feclude from the
world their younger children, in the hope of
difpofing of the elder ones.—" This alfo

is

is vanity."—It is well known that in Roman Catholic countries, moſt of the daughters are devoted to convents, to increaſe the fortunes of the elder ones.

In Proteſtant countries, though no vows are made, no confinement is exacted; yet nearly as many females are as much condemned to a ſtate of celibacy, as if they were ſhut up in a convent.

There are but a few men, comparatively, that will take for a wife, an amiable maiden, without a fortune ſuitable to his own. Every young man is taught to look out where he can marry to advantage; wealth is ſuppoſed to include every thing; and bodily charms and mental qualities, ſhrink to nothing before it. Thus the ugly, the deformed, the fooliſh, the diſtempered, are preferred with fortunes; while the lovely, the amiable, the accompliſhed, who are every way qualified to

G

be

be wives and mothers, are paſt by, neglected, deſpiſed, and forgotten.

It is allowed by all men, that women
ſtand in need of protectors in every ſtage
of their journey through life ; but when
they are thus circumſtanced, where are
they to find them ?

Brothers generally look on ſiſters as in-
cumbrances on families ; more remote relations ſeldom trouble themſelves about
them : without fortunes, without friends,
how can they ſuſtain—

> " Th' oppreſſor's wrong, the proud man's con-
>   tumely,
> " The pang of deſpis'd love, the law's delay,
> " The inſolence of office, and the ſpurn
> " That patient merit from th' unworthy takes."
>
> SHAKESPEARE.

But theſe are not all the injuries to
which ſingle and unprotected women are
liable. Thoſe who believe themſelves
poſſeſſed of wit, uſe it to turn them to

con-

contempt and ridicule; not becaufe they are unworthy, but becaufe they are unfortunate. There are few modern Comedies that do not give irrefragable proofs of this.—The Aunt Deborah's, and Mrs. Malaprop's, are the ftanding jeft of the modern writers; and even Mr. Cumberland, though a chafte and refined writer, has lent his hand to throw a ftone at fifters and aunts who are unmarried; whatever merit they may have, or whatever misfortunes they may have endured.

But there is *one* modern writer, who has gone ftill further than this infult; he has made ufe of the term *Old Maids!* as his vehicle, to convey to the public ear all his fatire and ridicule, upon ferious, and even facred fubjects. It is true, that he has fcattered in their way fome fugar-plums, and comfits, for the fifterhood, in order to conceal the poifon he has mixed for them;

but

but his malicious intention is eafily feen and detected.

I have by me, an extract from a letter which a friend of mine received from one of the firft writers in the kingdom, and which fhe permitted me to copy :

" The book you mention is altogether " execrable ; and I have the fatisfaction " of knowing, that it is execrated by all " who yet pretend to virtue or decency " among us."

Men who thus ufe their talents, derive neither honour nor advantage to themfelves ; on the contrary, thofe who have ftood forth in the behalf of the defenfelefs part of our fex, have, by refpecting them, become truly refpectable.

The names of Addifon, Richardfon, Thomas, Ruffel, Fordyce, Gregory, Percival, will always be remembered with honour, by the difcerning and the worthy

of

of both fexes ; for the female caufe is the caufe of virtue ; and, I truft, it will never want champions to fupport it.

That any women who defire to be thought virtuous themfelves, fhould join with men in ridiculing thofe of their own fex, merely becaufe they are unmarried, feems ftranger than any thing I have mentioned ; yet fuch women are to be found.

And why do you (I would fay) take plea-fure in cafting reflections upon old maids ? —that is, upon women who, not meeting with a fuitable eftablifhment, from various caufes and reafons, have neither difgraced themfelves nor their families ?

Every woman in this fituation muft be an old maid ; or fhe muft be fomething worfe. What then ; do you think the lat-ter ftate the moft honourable ? Would you wifh that your aunts, your fifters, your daughters, fhould think fo ? Would you

G 3   have

have them draw a ſtill ſtronger inference
from your contempt of the ſiſterhood,
againſt your own diſpoſition ?—Conſider
this—and bluſh at the reflection ; for you
have the greateſt cauſe, upon every account.

Leaving hatred, malice, and all un-
charitableneſs to the reproach of their
own hearts, in a ſerious hour ; and meek-
neſs and benevolence, to the ſilent rewards
of ſelf-approbation ; I will return to my
principal ſubject.

Though Proteſtants in general have a
rooted averſion to the name of a convent,
it is certain that there are many benefits
ariſing from theſe inſtitutions, as well as
inconveniences and abuſes ; particularly
to ſuch women as are forſaken by their
relatives, and deſerted by the world. It
has been thought by many perſons of
ſound judgment and liberal minds, that
it might be practicable to found a ſociety
that

that might retain all the good properties of these communities, and avoid all the bad ones. There are many women of small fortunes, with cultivated minds, and enlarged hearts, that would chuse to retire from the bustle of the world, and devote their time and talents to the benefit of others, rather than sink into *ennuï*, which always attends indolence. These might found an asylum for themselves, and a seminary of education for others.

I have worked upon this subject a long time ago, and will send you the result of my labour in the next pacquet.

The plan I have laid, will speak to several different classes of people, so that I shall not observe the gradations regularly, as I have done hitherto; but shall go through several together.

In the mean time I will reply to the other parts of your letter. I will endeavour to find out a proper person to be go-

vernefs

verneſs to the young ladies, your daughters; I do not expect to find one in the
country, but when I go to London I ſhall
hope to ſucceed; my friend, Mrs. Langſton, has a very large acquaintance, and
ſhe is very likely to aſſiſt me in this buſineſs. It ſeems to me, that the young
perſon who executes this office in your
ladyſhip's family, may ſuit Mrs. Strictland; ſhe is already pleaſed with the idea,
and I ſhall be happy to ſerve two deſerv-
ing perſons at the ſame time.

Mr. Balderſon is building at a great
rate; Mrs. Strictland is purchaſing houſes
in the village; ſhe has numbers every
day ſoliciting to be her tenants. She
wiſhes to realize Shenſtone's idea. If I
had a large fortune, I would build myſelf
a neighbourhood. There is a Novel built
upon this foundation, called " Shenſtone
Green." The outline is good, but the fil-
ling up is poor and unequal.

Mrs.

Mrs. Strictland will not suffer knaves and fools to take shelter in her territories; but she will invite the ingenious, the virtuous, and the unfortunate, and build for them a real paradise.

With my humble compliments and best wishes for all those most dear to your ladyship,

I am your obliged and faithful servant,

FRANCES DARNFORD.

P. S. Mrs. Strictland and Madame di Soranzo desire to present respectful compliments.

LETTER

LETTER XIV.

MRS. DARNFORD TO LADY A———.

I SEND, enclofed, my principal Plan for your ladyfhip's infpection.

F. D.

THE PLAN OF

A FEMALE COMMUNITY,

AND

A SEMINARY OF FEMALE EDUCATION.

THE defects of the prefent fyftem of female education in this country, are generally acknowledged, by all who have confidered and remarked upon it; they are, indeed, too apparent in the manners of Englifh women of the prefent times. —They have formerly been celebrated for

the

the modefty of their drefs and deport-
ment, for the purity and even fanctity of
their manners. It is believed that there
are ftill a great number of individuals,
who deferve and fupport the national character; but it is indifputable, that the
manners of our country women in general have fuftained a great and alarming
alteration in the courfe of the prefent
century.

The decreafe of marriages, the increafe
of divorces, the frequency of feparations,
bear melancholy teftimony to the truth of
thefe affertions. The great number of
public victims of pride, vanity, and diffipation, are too apparent and frequent, to
leave any doubt remaining of this general
declenfion of manners.

Among thofe refpectable women who
fuppott the national character, there are
many who lament this alarming alteration; who are ardently folicitous to ftop

G 6   the

the torrent of vice and folly, to inveſtigate the cauſes of it, and to ſeek out for a remedy.

They think this muſt be found in a better ſyſtem of education, by which the riſing generation may be preſerved from the contagion of bad example, and be en-abled to reſtore the national character of virtue, modeſty, and diſcretion.

It is certain, that the principal cauſes of this declenſion of manners, are, firſt, a bad method of education ; and, ſecond-ly, a ſeries of bad examples after this education is completed. Leaving the latter article to the inveſtigation of abler hands, we ſhall purſue the firſt, as the ob-ject of our preſent enquiry.

It is the general method of people of condition to give their children, from the ſtate of infancy, to the care of nurſes, and ſervants of a low claſs ; to perſons gene-rally ignorant and mercenary, frequently unprincipled.

unprincipled. Thefe preceptors prevent the feeds of virtue from germinating, and cultivate in the young and flexible heart the weeds of pride, felf-confequence, fraud, and artifice, and every bad propenfity.

Thofe parents can never be too highly honoured, who themfelves fuperintend the education of their children; for though they only fulfil their duties, yet, confidering the great numbers who neglect them, they are entitled to praife and refpect; there is no kind of education equal to that of a wife and virtuous mother; but this character is every day lefs common among us.

When the children are taken out of the nurfery, they are fent to fome fchool, where they are fuppofed to learn the rudiments of language, morals, and manners; every ufeful kind of knowledge, and every ornamental accomplifhment.—
Thefe

Thefe depend, however, upon the chance of the merit and abilities of the perfons who are intrufted with this very important charge.

When we confider how few perfons are duly qualified for this facred truft, we need not wonder at the mifchiefs arifing from the abufe in the difcharge of it; they have been remarked by many who have been fufferers by them, or who have felt their effects in thofe who were the moft dear to them.

It is not in this Effay, that we fhall enumerate thefe abufes and corruptions; none who think ferioufly are ignorant of them; we only juft hint the caufes and feek for the remedy.

When we confider the great increafe of boarding fchools, we ought not to be furprifed at the increafe of the evils arifing from them. In every town, village, or even hamlet, there are perfons to be found

who

who take upon them the great and important charge of female education : and over their doors are feen in letters of gold,

" *A Boarding School for Young Ladies.*"

Adventurers of all kinds have found refources in this profeffion : needy foreigners, without friends or characters; broken traders; ladies of doubtful virtue; ladies' waiting-maids; nay, even low and menial fervants, have fucceeded in raifing a boarding fchool. What muft we think of the negligence and credulity of fuch parents as intruft their moft precious treafures, their children, the facred depofits of heaven and their country, to the care of unknown—perhaps, ignorant, —perhaps, unprincipled people?

We do not mean to include all boarding fchools under this defcription; we know that there are fome, which anfwer every purpofe of virtuous and ingenuous education, fuch as we encourage and recommend;

mend ; but we infift, that far the greater number, are either ufelefs, or pernicious, efpecially to the lower claffes of people : and even among thofe of the better kinds, the attention is chiefly paid to external accomplifhments, while the moral duties, and the focial virtues are neglected, or flightly attended to.

How often do we fee the young girls come from thofe fchools, full of pride, vanity, and felf-confequence !—ignorant of the duties and virtues of a domeftic life, infolent to their inferiors, proud and faucy to their equals, impertinent to their parents ; without that fweet modefty and delicacy of mind and manners, which are the fureft guards of female virtue, and the beft omens of their future characters as wives, mothers, and miftreffes of families; and which nothing can compenfate for the want of.

To this fource, we have traced one of the

the great caufes of the prefent degeneracy of female manners, which our undertaking is intended to reform and to
remedy.

We conceive, that it is very practicable
to inculcate the higheft principles of religion and virtue, and to blend them with
the moft elegant female accomplifhments,
and the moft ufeful focial and domeftic
qualities; this, therefore, is the defign
and purpofe of our new plan of female
education : but this is not our only purpofe; we propofe to extend the advantages of it ftill further, to the general
utility of the whole community.

We have obferved from the increafe of
boarding fchools, and from the general
ftile of education among the middling
and lower ranks of people, every degree
educating their children in a way above
their prefent circumftances, and future expectations;

pectations ; that a great number of young
women come into the world without fortunes fuitable to their educations, and afterwards, by the death or mifconduct of
their friends, are expofed to all the dangers of a deferted and friendlefs fituation.
—Their parents are, perhaps, juftly punifhed for their vanity and ambition ; but,
furely, the unfortunate fufferers are the
objects of our tendereft pity ; and if they
fall into errors of conduct, we fhould
reflect, that their faults are not ori-
ginally their own. How often are they
feduced by defigning men ! or become the
victims of their own credulity and inno-
cence. How are they fhunned and in-
fulted by thofe who never experienced
their trials. The retrofpect is painful ;—
and it is increafed by the confideration of
the numbers of victims thus facrificed.—
Among thefe, we find the daughters of
indigent

indigent clergymen, of officers in the army and navy, of placemen of all kinds, and, in short, of all whose incomes depend on their lives, and who generally leave their children unprovided for.

Our present undertaking is partly designed to provide for these helpless, friendless, destitute young women, to take them from the dangers that surround them, to give them habits of industry and employment, to give them some business for their future support, and, finally, to make them useful and happy members of society.

These, and many other noble and useful purposes, are designed in this our Plan of Female Education, which is here offered to the public consideration; if they appear worthy of encouragement, it is hoped they will meet with the assistance necessary to carry so great a design into execution;

we

we claim the patronage and protection of
the virtuous and generous, and we despise
the attacks of the ignorant and malig-
nant censurers of our Plan, confcious
of the rectitude and integrity of our intentions.

Influenced by the confiderations abovementioned, feveral Ladies of unqueftionable characters and abilities, have determined to form a community, for the
purpose of founding a Seminary of Female Education upon the following Plan :

They will enter into a voluntary engagement for three years, to be renewed
at the end of the term ; or, in cafe any
perfon choofes to be releafed from her
engagement, fhe may then be freed from
it.

They will each fubfcribe a certain part
of their refpective fortunes, for the fup-

port

port and fervice of the faid Community.

The Community thus united, fhall hire or purchafe a large and commodious houfe, in a convenient fituation; at a limited diftance from a market town, but not in it; which they fhall furnifh and prepare for the reception of boarders.

Each of the Ladies fhall apply for the particular department which fhe defires to undertake; and her pretentions fhall be examined, and decided by the majority of the Community.

As foon as every department is filled up, the Ladies fhall hold a Council every Monday morning, to compofe the Rules for governing the Society, and to confult on the beft methods of putting them into execution.

The

*The Offices of the Ladies of the Female
Community.*

I. THE Superior, or Governefs of the
Community, who fhall be the head
of it, fhe fhall have two votes on
every queftion, and many privileges to be explained hereafter.

II. The Treafurer, who fhall receive and
difburfe the revenue of the Community, and give a regular account of it.

III. The Superintendent of the House-
hold, who fhall regulate and in-
fpect every department in it.

IV. The Governefs of the Young Pupils,
who fhall direct their morals, manners, and ftudies.

V. The Sub-Governefs, who fhall fuperintend all their works, and con-
ftantly attend in the fchool at certain hours.

VI. The

VI. The House-keeper, who shall order in all the provisions, direct the tables, and keep the weekly account.

VII. The Intendent of the Garden, and all its productions.

VIII. The Intendent of the Cellar, and the Liquors of all Kinds, and who keeps an account of them.

IX. The Intendent of all the Works done in the Community, particularly those made and sold for the benefit of the poor young women in it.

X. The Secretary to the Community, who shall write all the letters in the name of it, and keep a journal of all the transactions in it from its foundation.

XI. The Accomptant, who shall keep a Ledger, and enter an account of the receipts and disbursements.

XII. The Intendent of the Dairy and Poultry-

Poultry-yard, who fhall keep an account of their Productions.

After the Community fhall be eftablifhed, there fhall be as many young ladies received and educated, as can be accommodated. They fhall be the children of people of good fortune, who will be expected to pay a handfome price for their board. They fhall have every advantage of the beft education, without any of the dangers of a common boarding fchool.—The ftricteft attention fhall be paid to their moral, and mental, as well as perfonal improvements; and they fhall be taught every branch of ufeful knowledge in common life, to qualify them to govern and conduct a family.

Thefe young ladies muft, in all refpects conform to the Rules of the Community, and they muft have every thing they wear made by the fervants of it.

It

It is propofed, that all kinds of work for the ufe of the Community, fhall be done within its own walls.

It is propofed, that a certain number of young girls, the daughters of clergymen, officers in the army and navy, placemen, or any profeffion whofe parents have died in indigent circumftances, and left them entirely deftitute of any provifion, fhall be received into this community for the term of feven years; to be employed in the fervice of it during that time; and if their behaviour is approved, they fhall receive proper teftimonials, and other tokens of approbation, in proportion to the ability of the Community to confer them, in order to promote their eftablifhment in their refpective bufinefs or employment.

During the time of their refidence in the Community, they fhall receive all the advantages of tuition which are given to the

H pupils

pupils of condition, and fhall be conftant-
ly employed in their affigned departments;
and every one fhall learn a trade, or bufinefs, for their future fupport and provifion.

There fhall be one of each bufinefs here
mentioned :

1.—The Milliner to the Community, and
      teacher of her art.

2.—The Mantua-maker, and teacher of
      the fame.

3.—The Clear-ftarcher, and teacher of the
      fame.

4.—The Lace-maker, and teacher.

5.—The Stay-maker, and teacher.

6.—Embroiderer, and teacher of curious
      works.

7.—Plain-worker, and teacher.

8.—Spinner of hemp and flax, and teacher.

9.—Knitter of thread, cotton, and worf-
      ted hofe, &c.

10.—The

10.—The Florift, who makes flowers, and
draws patterns for work.

11.—Affiftant to the Sub-governefs, and
teacher in the fchool.

12.—Second Affiftant to the fame, and
teacher.

13.—Affiftant to the Houfe-keeper.

14.—Affiftant to the Intendent of the
Dairy, &c.

If there fhould be room for more, the
reft muft be occafional affiftants to the
Community, in whatever department they
may be wanted, and fucceed to the trades
as the elder ones leave the Community.

In order to avoid every incitement to
pride, vanity, and felf-conceit, it is propofed, that all the young pupils of this
Community fhall be cloathed in a neat
plain uniform ; and that neatnefs in the
wearing it, fhall be the only mark of diftinction.

H 2 The

The Affiftants to wear an inferior uniform.

The fervants, another uniform of inferior materials.

No kind of diftinction fhall be fhewn to children of birth, fortune, or any accidental advantages.

It is propofed, that rewards fhall be given to all who diftinguifh themfelves in any particular department, and that marks of approbation fhall be given publicly, at ftated times of the year, to encourage the young pupils to deferve them.

Each of the Affiftants fhall have a certain portion of time allotted them to work for the benefit of the community, and the money arifing from this allotment, fhall be employed for the purpofe of fettling the Affiftants, when they are fent into the world; either as a marriage portion, or to eftablifh them in their refpective bufineffes.

The

The young ladies are to be encouraged
to devote some part of their time to this
laudable purpose, but at their own option,
that they may have the full merit of it.

It will be neceſſary to appoint a Chaplain to the Community, and to have a
Chapel within the houſe. The Chaplain
to attend on Sundays and holydays, but
not to reſide in the houſe.

One of the Ladies, Governeſſes of the
Community, ſhall read prayers every
morning at ſtated hours. The prayers
ſhall be ſelected from the Liturgy of the
Church of England, with ſuch other oc-
caſional ones as ſhall be appointed by the
Superior.

The ſervants of the Community ſhall
be choſen from the induſtrious poor, or
ſuch perſons as have ſuffered by misfortunes. It is preſumed that ſuch perſons
being under particular obligations to the

H 3 Community,

Community, would be likely to ferve it faithfully.

All the fervants in the houfe fhall, at leifure hours, fpin flax and hemp for the ufe of the Community; and every one fhall be allowed an hour every day, to fpin for their own benefit; the money fo earned to be faved for them, and to be paid, with the intereft, when they leave the Community, to fupport them in age and ficknefs.

It is alfo propofed, that two vifiting days fhall be allowed every week; one for morning vifitors, who fhall be received in a parlour, appropriated to that purpofe; where the Superior, or fuch of the ladies as are appointed by her, fhall do the honours of the houfe.

None of the Pupils or Affiftants fhall receive or fend any letters, without the infpection of one or more of the ladies of the Community

Every

Every perfon who defires to vifit the Community, or any of the Pupils of it, muft give notice, by a written note to the Superior a week before, and receive an anfwer appointing the time.

There fhall be a porter, a footman, a gardener, an errand-man, attending the Community; and all the men fervants fhall be lodged out of the houfe, but within the hearing of the houfe-bell at the top of it.

The Community fhall hire or purchafe lands contiguous to it, for every convenient purpofe. It is prefumed that they will keep cows, to furnifh their houfe with butter, cheefe, milk, and cream.—They may alfo keep hogs to very good account; alfo poultry of all kinds, to fupply the table; and to have every poffible conveniency within themfelves.

The Weekly Council fhall extend thefe hints, and form them into Rules; and

H 4 fhall

fhall add fuch further regulations as fhall be judged neceffary and proper for their fervice.

Every perfon defirous to promote or affift in this undertaking, fhall fend their names and refidence to the perfons and places, to be hereafter appointed.

N. B. Notice will be given in the public papers, when this Plan is near being put into execution.

The above Plan might be much farther extended; and under the Patronage of fome Lady of diftinguifhed Rank and Character, become a confirmed inftitution.

It is fuppofed, that ladies in the firft year of their widowhood—Ladies, whofe hufbands are fent abroad in public offices —Single ladies, who have not fettled their plan of life—Ladies of more advanced age, who have met with misfortunes or difappointments, and wifh to retire from the

the world:—It is fuppofed, that many ladies of thefe, or other fituations, would be glad to retire to fuch an afylum.

They fhould not be admitted for lefs than a year; they muft be people of un-fpotted characters. They fhould pay a good price for their board, and upon find-ing every requifite for paffing their time agreeably, it is prefumed, that from thefe might arife future benefactreffes to the Society.

Hints for the Government of the Female Community.

EVERY perfon who defires to be ad-mitted into the Community, fhall give in her name at a certain time, to be appoint-ed, with the fums fhe will advance and fettle towards maintaining it.

The firft twelve perfons fhall compofe the Sifterhood; and to fucceed in turn to the office of fuperior, in preference to any that fhall afterwards be admitted.

H 5 Every

Every one of the Sifters fhall advance, at the leaft, one hundred pounds for the outfet ; and fhall pay, yearly, twenty pounds into the treafury of this Society. —It is fuppofed that it will, in due time, maintain itfelf, and provide for others. If every petty boarding fchool can fupport itfelf, furely an undertaking of fo much greater extent, contrived with a view to the public utility, may do more.

A large and commodious houfe fhall be bought or hired for the purpofes of the Community ; it fhould be within a few miles of a good market town, for the fupply of all things wanted for the ufes of the Community.

The houfe fhould be fitted up under the direction of the Superior, who fhall be chofen as foon as the number of twelve is completed.

A Council of the Sifterhood fhall be held every Monday morning, at ten o'clock, o'clock, to confult on the beft method of putting the Rules into execution; and afterwards for the well-governing of the Community.

Each of the Sifters fhall apply to the reft, for the particular department fhe propofes to undertake; the pretentions to be decided by the majority. The Superior fhall have two votes.

When every department is filled up, and the Sifterhood are ready to undertake their refpective offices, public notice fhall be given in the papers, and propofals fhould be printed for A New Seminary of Female Education; the advantages to be received from it fhould be fet forth, the terms offered, and the time appointed to receive the young pupils; in the mean time the Sifterhood fhall engage the proper Affiftants, and all other perfons to be employed in the fervice of the Community.

H 6

In

In the country, the pupils muft not pay lefs than thirty pounds a year, and two guineas entrance ; but thofe near the capital, muft pay fifty pounds a year, and five guineas entrance ; as all the teachers muft be paid in the fame proportion ; all other expences are to be included of all kinds whatfoever.

All the teachers in the Seminary are to be females, whether of dancing, drawing, mufic, language, &c.

The pupils may alfo be taught, if required, clear-ftarching, ironing, paftry, confectionary, cookery, &c. at the defire of their parents or guardians.

All the young pupils are to have every thing they wear made in the Community, by the young perfons engaged in its fervice.

It is fuppofed, that all the poor young maidens, educated in the Community, are, at their difmiffion, to have a marriage portion,

portion, or elfe to be fet up in their refpective bufineffes.

Each of the Affiftants is to have a
young perfon under them, in training to
their particular art, and as a fucceffor to
them, whenever they fhall leave the Community.

When the Community fhall have raifed
a fund fufficient, the intereft of it is to be
appropriated to the Affiftants, to provide
for them, and to procure them an eftablifhment; and all the extra works done
in the Community fhall be devoted to
this purpofe. Every Sunday after morning fervice, there fhall be a collection of
alms, for the relief of the unfortunate
poor.

Every fervant in the Community fhall
be allowed an hour every evening to work
for themfelves, and another hour to
earn fomething to lay by for themfelves,
when they fhall be difmiffed.

The

The Superior fhall be called the Mother of the Community.

The Sifterhood, by the name of Sifter, with the proper addition.

The Affiftants, by their proper names, without any addition.

The Young Pupils, Mifs, or Mademoifelle, with their proper names.

The Superior, or one of the Sifterhood by her appointment, fhall read prayers twice every day ; at ten o'clock in the morning, and at eight in the evening, when all the Community (except fuch as cannot be fpared from their refpective offices) are to attend.

The prayers fhall be felected from the Liturgy of the Church of England, with fuch other prayers as fhall be felected by the Superior ; thofe of Bifhop Hoadly are recommended.

The houfe-bell fhall toll five minutes

to

to give notice of prayers, and all that attend, muſt come exactly to the time.

While the Community is in its infancy, it muſt go on Sundays to the pariſh church, where ſeats muſt be appropriated, or, perhaps built for them ; but when it is grown too large to be accommodated, it will be proper to ſolicit the patronage of the Biſhop of the Dioceſe, to honour him with the title of its Protector, and to requeſt him to appoint a Chaplain to the Community.

The Superior ſhall on Wedneſdays and Fridays, either before or after prayers, read an exhortation to thoſe who attend, upon the religious, moral, and ſocial duties, and enforce the ſtricteſt obſervance of them; ſhe may ſelect from the works of the beſt writers, or occaſionally give obſervations of her own.

There ſhall be a room appointed for a ſchool-room, another for the refectory.—

The

The pupils fhall dine at an early hour, fuppofe one o'clock, and then return to the fchool room; after they rife, the Teachers and Affiftants fhall fit down at the fame table, and then all retire to the fchool room, or walk in the garden with the pupils, if the weather permits; and all of them fhall be allowed an hour for exercife and amufement before they return to their work; and the fame before dinner. —There fhall be a fecond dinner ready at three o'clock for the Boarders and the Sifterhood, excepting fuch of them as fhall choofe to dine early, and fuch as are appointed to prefide over the early tables, which fhall be taken in rotation by all the Sifterhood, excepting the Superior.

Some of the fervants fhall dine after the early tables, others after the late ones, as they can be fpared from their offices.

The hours of the Pupils, Teachers, and Affiftants, fhall be regulated, and ftated

hours

hours appointed for tuition, exercife, play, &c.

When the rules of the Community are eftablifhed, certain penalties fhall be enjoined for every infringement of them.—If any Pupil, Teacher, Affiftant, or Servant, fhall commit a fault of confequence, the Superior fhall reprove her privately for the firft offence; for the fecond, before the whole Sifterhood; for the third, fhe fhall be expelled the Community.

If any of the Sifterhood fhall defire to leave the Community, fhe fhall declare it, and her reafons, before the Sifterhood; and if fully refolved to go, fhe fhall be releafed by the Superior, and another chofen to fupply her place; and if any of them fhould behave fo as to give offence to all the reft, fhe fhould be exhorted by the Superior to amend, or elfe to withdraw from the Community; and the reafons fhall not be declared, or known, except to

the

the Sifterhood, fo that her retreat fhall appear to be voluntary, to the reft of the Community.

All thofe perfons who perufe this Plan, and are inclined to encourage it, are defired to propofe fuch improvements as they can fuggeft, means of reducing it to practice, and rules for the well-governing the propofed Community.

LETTER XV.

LADY A——, TO MRS. DARNFORD.

YOUR Plans, my dear friend, have afforded me much entertainment, and much matter for reflection. Be you angry or pleafed, I could not forbear communicating them to my Lord.

It is eafy to fee by your brevity, and by your gliding through the fubject, when ever you are obliged to fpeak of him, that you have not cordially forgiven the affronts you received from him; but I flatter myfelf that I fhall have the honour and pleafure to reconcile you together, and that he fhall be your true friend, and the fervant of your virtues, for the remainder of your lives.—You muft not deny me this favour; my heart is fet upon it; and if I cannot effect it, I fhall be grieved and difappointed; in

fhort,

fhort, I fhall be fick, and I cannot fay what may not happen to me.

My Lord has a great and real efteem for 'you, and though he always thought highly of you, he did not imagine you had ever thought fo deeply upon fubjects of public utility and importance.

He honours and admires you for your liberality and benevolence, and you will have the benefit of his remarks upon your writings, which will be of infinitely more fervice to you, than any thing I can fay, in return for your valuable prefent.

You are to underftand, however, that in giving my Lord's opinion, I give you alfo my own, expreffed to advantage; and that I referve to myfelf a right to add whatever I pleafe without his feeing it.

All your Plans are expreffive of humanity and benevolence, but your laft fhows a knowledge of mankind, and endeavours

to

to contribute to a reformation of the manners of the times.

The only doubt is of the practicability : is it possible to draw together twelve women all of one mind ?—Will they unite in the executive parts you have allotted them? —I heartily wish that such Communities could be established;. but I fear the passions and prejudices of both sexes, would unite to depreciate the scheme, and to defeat your designs.

My Lord says, that your chief labours are for your own sex, and that you have not given so much attention to the other; he desires to know your opinions of the best education for boys, and particularly on the great question yet undecided, whether public or private education is the best? He hopes you will further enlarge on that of both sexes in the upper ranks of life. —I am convinced that your philanthropy extends to all ranks and degrees.—If I

harboured

harboured a doubt, your kind attention to the young woman who at prefent is the companion to my daughters, would remove it, for it is inexpreffibly kind in you to think of her, a perfon unknown to you, and only mentioned accidentally.

When we meet in London, we will fettle all thefe points, and I will meet you upon your own ground, and try which of us fhall get the better in acts of friendfhip and generofity.

The winter comes on apace; when may I expect you in town ?—You may bring up the reft of your papers; for though I value your correfpondence in a very high degree, I hold the opinion of M. Marivaux, that the fociety of people of genius is fuperior to their writings, and I long for your company.—Do not fuppofe from what I have faid, that I mean to acquit you of your promife ;—by no means.—Continue your tranfcripts, and bring your fubject

ject fairly to a conclufion. Write to me till you come to London. Though I am impatient to fee you, I will not difpenfe with one line of your writings.

All that are dear to me wifh to be fo to you, but efpecially

Your obliged and affectionate friend,

LOUISA A——.

LETTER

LETTER XVI.

MRS. DARNFORD TO LADY A————.

WHAT shall I say to Lady A————, who continues, in defiance of my remonstrances, to shew my letters to her Lord, and to convey his remarks and further expectations to me?—Her conduct reminds me of what Miss Grandison says to Miss Byron, and in her words will I reprove Lady A———— :

" No married woman will 1 trust with what lies in
" the innermost fold of my heart. Their husbands are
" always the wiser for what they know ; and they,
" becoming both tempters and accusers, laugh at us,
" and make it wonderful for a woman to keep a
" secret."

GRANDISON, Vol. I. Letter 37.

But reproof and remonstrance signify nothing ; you still persevere, and still hold me to my promise. I must say that you are arbitrary ; but though I murmur, I obey.

There

There is one circumſtance in your conduct that gives me pleaſure, as it proves
the entire confidence that ſubſiſts between
you and your Lord. It is difficult to
withhold any thing from thoſe we love
beſt; and in happy marriages it can hardly
be otherwiſe.

I cannot yet come to town. I have let-
lers from Captain Maurice, whom you will
remember as the perſecutor of Madame
di Soranzo. He promiſes to meet me there
in February. I ſhall carry his ward, Miſs
Brady, with me, as he wiſhes to ſee her.
—He has promiſed to reſign all pretentions to the property of Donna Iſabella;
and if ſhe requires it, he will join with
her in the ſale of her eſtate at D—. Mrs.
Strictland has urged us ſo warmly and ſo
kindly to be her neighbours, that we have
conſented; ſhe is fitting up a houſe which
ſhe has lately purchaſed for us, and her
houſe is to be our home till it is ready to

I   receive

receive us. I have offered to accompany
Donna Isabella to Naples, if she would
prefer a final settling there. Her answer
was this:—" Not unless you will stay
with me there; your company is the first
blessing of my life, and nothing shall in-
duce me to part with it. I will say with
the widowed Naomi, — " Thy people
shall be my people, and thy God shall be
my God."—She wept while she spoke;
and embracing me, demanded, if I wished
to send her from me.—I assured her, that
I only meant it as a trial of her own inclination, before we removed to a new ha-
bitation; and that I would never leave
her, but at her own desire. She said—
" then nothing but death shall ever part
us."—I renewed my promise to her.

Miss Brady is uneasy lest her guardian
should take her from me. I tell her she has
no reason for this apprehension; Miss Strictland and she have commenced an early
friend-

friendfhip, which I approve, and hope it will laft to the end of their lives;—they fear nothing fo much as being feparated. Patty Martin is my adopted daughter; it is incumbent on me to provide for her, as I have taken her away from her family. I am the fteward and manager for thefe three perfons, and my tendereft cares and attentions are devoted to them.

I have many things to do for their fervice, and I muft order my coming to town fo as will be moft convenient for this purpofe. I have written to Mrs. Langfton, and told her my reafons for delaying my coming till after Chriftmas; fhe gives a reluctant acquiefcence.

In the interim, I fhall have leifure to tranfcribe the reft of my papers, to fulfil my promife to your Ladyfhip, and to conclude all that I mean to fay upon the fubject.

I find myfelf obliged to reply to fome

things

things in your laft favour : I do not take to myfelf the firft claim to my principal plan; it is extracted from thofe who have gone before me; but I have endeavoured to prune away all the romantic and impracticable parts, and only to retain what is reafonable and practicable.—I do not fee why twelve women may not agree under the direction of one fuperior. If they were all to be equal in power, it might create a jealoufy; but under an acknowledged fuperior, they would fubmit to be governed.

In all communities, little or great, there muft be a head; and this point once fettled, is fettled for ever. There are actually fuch communities in many parts of the world; I have been told there have been more than one in England in the prefent century. I could wifh that one fuch was eftablifhed in every county, and that all other boarding fchools were annihilated.

hilated. I have thoughts of laying this
Plan before the public, and taking their
judgment upon it.

I confeſs that my chief labours are for
my own fex; I confider it as a duty to
them; nevertheleſs, when this taſk is per-
formed, I will venture a few remarks for
the other.

Though I have ſpoken againſt boarding
ſchools in general, I am convinced that
there are fome that are what they ought
to be; and there are many young people
in fituations that make it proper and even
neceſſary to place them where they may
receive the advantages of a liberal education. Young girls who are deprived of their
mothers, and have no relations that can or
will ſupply the mother's place—Thofe who
come to good fortunes unexpectedly, and
want to be qualified to fupport them properly—Thofe whofe fathers marry again,
(for it is feldom that a mother-in-law will

I 3   take

take the trouble of the childrens' education.)

Many young Ladies are fent from the
East and West Indies to receive education
in England, and (till my feminaries are
established) it is neceffary there fhould be
fchools for them. It is much to be wifhed,
that in thefe fchools they would pay more
attention to morals and principles than to
ornamental qualities.

It is not fufficient that they learn nothing wrong, that they are kept from evil
of every kind; they fhould be taught,
that all their happinefs, prefent and future, depends upon virtue; their moral,
focial, and relative duties, fhould be
ftrongly and frequently inculcated, and
rewards and punifhments given with a
view to thefe, rather than to fuperficial
accomplifhments. Pride and vanity are
weeds that grow more or lefs in all human
hearts, they fhould be checked, where
they

they are moſt encouraged. Simplicity of
dreſs and manners ſhould be eſtabliſhed.
—I ſhould recommend a plain and neat
uniform for the ſcholars, to prevent the
emulation of vanity in them; there ſhould
be a perfect equality obſerved in the treatment of them, and no kind of reſpect
paid to ſuperior birth or fortune.

There is a line of beauty in every thing
—a medium between a low and ſordid ſtile
of dreſs, and the wild extravagancies of faſ-
ſhion. Among the genteel kind of Qua-
kers who have emerged from the original ſtiffneſs of that ſect, I have frequently obſerved that neatneſs and ele-
gance, that conſtitutes the true *ſimplex
munditii*; like real beauty, it has ſtruck
the eyes of all that beheld it, and has ex-
torted applauſe even from thoſe who were
determined not to follow it. A woman
of refined taſte, who adapts the faſhions

I 4   to

to her perſon, rather than her perſon to the faſhions, will always be more admired than ſhe whoſe perſon is overwhelmed with them.

It is time enough when young ladies are taken from ſchool, to let them be initiated into the myſteries of faſhion; perhaps they may, by that time, have acquired a bias in favour of ſimplicity of dreſs and manners that may attend them through life.

And now, my dear Lady A——, I am going to give you a Plan of Education, extracted from my principal one, by the deſire of a lady, who has actually proved it to be practicable by putting it into practice.——She did me the honour to invite me to take a ſhare of it; but having eſcaped from the inconveniencies of my former ſituation, and being engaged in a different walk, I declined it. I have a very high opinion of this lady, and think

think her every way qualified for the undertaking.

Leaving this Plan to your confideration,

I remain,

Your Ladyſhip's obedient ſervant,

F. DARNFORD.

THE PLAN OF

A SEMINARY OF FEMALE EDUCATION,

Which was opened at Tottenham, Middlesex,

BY MRS. M. SCRIVEN.

IN THE YEAR 1788.

———

" THE defects of the prefent fyftem
" of Female Education are generally ac-
" knowledged by all who think ferioufly
" upon this important fubject : they are
" too apparent in the manners of the wo-
" men of thefe times.

" Englifh Ladies have been celebrated,
" above any in Europe, for the modefty
" of their drefs ;—the purity, and even
" fanctity, of their manners. There are
" many individuals who fuftain the na-
" tional reputation ; but yet it is evi-
" dent, that the manners of our country-
                                    " women

" women, in general, exhibit a great and
" alarming alteration within the pre-
" fent century. The moſt common ob-
" ferver cannot but fee and lament the
" public victims of pride, vanity, and
" folly ; to fay nothing of the train
" of more deſtructive vices which have
" difgraced the annals of female cha-
" racter within the laſt fifty years -
" thefe are too notorious to leave any
" room to doubt the truth of the prefent
" declenfion of manners in this country.

" Thofe honourable and worthy exam-
" ples who fupport and affert the national
" character, perceive and lament this
" alarming alteration, are folicitous to in-
" veftigate the caufes of it, and to feek
" for a remedy : they ardently feek to
" ſtop the progrefs of vice and folly : to
" preferve the rifing generation from the
" contagion of bad example ; the abfur-
" dities arifing from a falfe education ;

I 6 " and

" and to reftore the national character of
" virtue, modefty, and difcretion. Un-
" der the patronage of thefe moft refpect-
" able Ladies we prefume to offer to
" the public an attempt to rectify fome of
" thofe errors which have been fanctified
" by cuftom ; and have, therefore, long
" paffed unnoticed.

" The firft caufe of this national de-
" cline of manners, arifes from a bad me-
" thod of education : the fecond, from
" bad examples after this education is
" finifhed.—Leaving the latter to thofe
" whofe province it is to correct the mo-
" rals of the age, we confine ourfelves
" to the firft article.—

" People of condition give up their
" children very early to the care of fer-
" vants and nurfes : perfons generally ig-
" norant and uninformed, frequently un-
" principled, who prevent the feeds of
" future virtues from germinating, and
" bring

" bring forward the weeds of pride, felf-
" will, artifice, and every bad paffion and
" propenfity. From the nurfery they are
" fent to fchool, where they are fuppofed
" to learn the rudiments of morals, man-
" ners, every ufeful virtue, and every
" ornamental accomplifhment : but all
" muft depend upon the perfons to whofe
" care they are entrufted. When we con-
" fider how very few are duly qualified
" for this facred truft, we need not won-
" der at the mifchiefs that arife from the
" mifconduct, or abufes in the difcharge
" of it. They are fuch as have often
" been remarked upon by thofe who have
" been fufferers by them ; or by thofe
" who have feen and felt the effects of
" them upon any in whofe fate they
" were interefted. It is not in this little
" effay that we mean to enumerate them ;
" none who think ferioufly, can be igno-
        " rant

" rant of them; we fhall only juft point
" out the caufes, and then feek for a re-
" medy for thofe evils.

" When we confider the great increafe
" of common boarding-fchools, we fhall
" not be furprifed at the numerous mif-
" chiefs arifing from them. In every
" town, village, and even hamlet, there
" is one or more perfons who take upon
" themfelves the great and important
" charge of female education : over their
" doors may be feen in letters of gold,
" A Boarding School for Young Ladies.

" Adventurers of all kinds have found
" refources in this profeffion. Needy
" foreigners, without friends or recom-
" mendation,—ladies' upper fervants,—
" broken traders,—ladies of loft reputa-
" tion,—nay, even menial fervants, have
" fucceeded in raifing fchools of this
" kind : what muft we think of the negligence

" ligence and credulity of fuch parents,
" who intruft their moft precious trea-
" fures, their children, the facred depo-
" fits of heaven and their country, to the
" care of an unknown, ignorant, and,
" too frequently, unprincipled people;
" who return them back in a ftate that
" often obliges them to wifh them igno-
" rant of all that they have learned?—
" We do not, however, mean to include
" all boarding-fchools under this defcrip-
" tion. We know that there are fome
" that anfwer every purpofe of ingenu-
" ous and virtuous education; fuch as we
" wifh to promote and recommend; but
" we ftill infift, that there are far more
" that are either pernicious, or fall very
" fhort of the advantages expected from
" them.

" Among thofe of the better kinds,
" the attention is chiefly, if not en-
" tirely, directed to external accomplifh-
                              " ments;

" ments; while the moral duties and fo-
" cial virtues are neglected.—We daily
" fee young people come from thefe
" fchools, filled with pride, vanity, and
" felf-confequence;—ignorant of every
" neceſſary duty, and every uſeful qua-
" lity in domeſtic life;—infolent to their
" equals and inferiors; rejecting every kind
" of reftraint; and void of that modefty,
" humility, and delicacy of mind, which
" are the fureft guards of female vir-
" tue, and the beft pledges of their fu-
" ture conduct in life, as wives, mothers,
" and worthy members of fociety.

" Having traced thefe evils to their
" fources, we fhall offer to the public our
" beft endeavours towards a remedy for
" them.

" We conceive that it is practicable
" to inculcate the higheft principles of
" religion and virtue, and to blend them
" with the moft elegant and moft ufeful
" female

" female accomplifhments; and this is
" our aim in offering to the public our
" plan of female education.

" With thefe important objects con-
" ftantly in view (under the fanction of
" many ladies the moft refpectable; of
" rank, fortune, and character) feveral
" ladies of unblemifhed characters and
" unqueftionable abilities, fome of whom
" have had the honour of educating
" young ladies of the firft diftinction,
" and can produce credentials of indif-
" putable authority, have determined to
" open a Seminary of Education, upon
" a plan different from any boarding-
" School, in many refpects, in a pleafant
" and healthy fituation; within fuch a
" diftance from London, as will enfure
" the attendance of the beft mafters of
" all kinds.

THE

THE TERMS.

" For boarding, wafhing &c. learning
" grammatically the French, Englifh,
" and Italian languages ; the belles-let-
" tres ; the ufe of the globes ; hiftory,
" mufic, dancing, finging, drawing, and
" painting ; every ufeful and fafhionable
" kind of needle-work ; books, threads,
" tapes, needles, and every other necef-
" fary, FIFTY POUNDS a year.—Holi-
" days twice a year, Chriftmas and Mid-
" fummer :—at the latter there will be a
" public examination of the young pu-
" pils, by perfons of approved judg-
" ment and ability, and rewards given
" to diftinguifhed merit in every depart-
" ment.

" Each child fhall have a feparate bed ;
" and in cafe of ficknefs, proper apart-
" ments in a part of the houfe, un-
connected,

" connected, with the reft of it ; every
" medical affiftance, and proper at-
" tendance.

" In order to extend the benefits of
" this Seminary, it is propofed to ad-
" mit young ladies, who, either from
" want of opportunity, or neglect of
" the means of inftruction, are under
" the neceffity of applying for it at
" a later feafon of life, and who have
" objections to mixing with pupils
" younger than themfelves. Upon thefe
" confiderations, the Ladies are deter-
" mined to receive fuch boarders, if
" they can conform to the rules of the
" houfe.

" Such perfons fhall receive all the ad-
" vantages, without being obliged to at-
" tend the claffes ; and perfons, duly qua-
" lified, will be appointed to attend them
" in their own apartments, to give them
" private

" private leffons, and every inftruction
" they can require.

" They fhall pay FIFTY POUNDS a
" year, finding their own wine, fire, can-
" dles, and wafhing.

" N. B. No money to teachers or fer-
" vants."

LETTER

LETTER XVII.

MRS. DARNFORD TO LADY A——.

YOUR Ladyſhip already knows my opinions concerning the education of females of rank and fortune; and I am ſo happy as to know that you agree with me, that it is beſt to have a governeſs for them, under the eye and ſuperintendency of a mother. Maſters of all kinds may be had at proper times; and their education may be completed at home.

But there is an error predominant in our days—that of bringing them out too early, which both parents and children generally find cauſe to repent of.—They are ſeen too much, and too often, and made cheap in the eyes of men. I fear it much oftener promotes celibacy than marriage.

Mothers,

Mothers, 'tis faid, in days of old,
Efteem'd their girls more choice than gold.
Too well a daughter's worth they knew,
To make her cheap by public view.
None who their diamonds' value weigh,
Expofe thofe diamonds every day.
Then, when Sir Plume drew near and fmil'd,
The parent trembled for her child;
The firft advance alarm'd her breaft,
And fancy pick'd out all the reft.—
But now, no mother fears a foe,
No daughter fhudders at a beau.

COTTON's VISIONS.

Another error I fhall mention, is that
of allowing young girls to receive company, and return vifits by themfelves.—
How can they improve by the company
of thofe of their own age? On the contrary, it renders the fociety of thofe further advanced in life irkfome to them,
and lays a foundation for that difrefpect
to old age which is the certain criterion
of a declenfion of manners, and which is
to be feen too often in thefe days. Young
ladies ought not to receive company but
in the prefence of their mother or governefs;

nefs; nor fhould it be permitted too often even upon thefe terms.

Falfe indulgence is the ruin of more young people, than too much reftraint.— I was arguing this point one day with a lady, who maintained that I could not be a competent judge of this, becaufe I was not a mother. I replied, that I was the more likely to be unbiaffed; but I will give, faid I, another and ftronger reafon againft falfe indulgence.—I never knew a perfon of either fex that was grateful to the parent who fpoiled them: on the contrary, they always lay the blame of all their faults at that perfon's door. I refer this truth to your Ladyfhip's confideration. I believe it to be unanfwerable.

In the time of infancy and childhood, an implicit obedience fhould be exacted; this fpares much trouble both to the child and parent. I have feen a child and its parents contending for the fame points every

every day : but a habit of obedience pre-
vents all altercation, and the child is made
happier than it would be otherwise.—This
habit continues after the reftraint is abated;
as reafon gathers ftrength, what pleafure,
what pride does the child feel at being
admitted to the friendfhip of the parents,
to converfe with them freely, to be convinced that they were only reftrained for
their own benefit ! and till reafon fhould
come to their aid, what love, what refpect
will they feel for their parents !—This habit of obedience confirmed and eftablifhed
by reafon, will rather increafe than leffen,
and will continue all their lives. Nothing
can be more difagreeable than an hu-
moured child, who thinks itfelf the firft
perfon in company, and expects every
kind of attention, while it pays none to
any.—One of thefe was in a party that
went to the houfe of an eminent painter :
the company talked of the pictures, and
criticifed

criticifed them ;—the child was uneafy and diffatisfied ; at laft it faid to its aunt, I wifh we were gone away from this houfe ; nobody talks to me; nobody takes notice of me. A polite and agreeable child, on the contrary, pays every attention to others, and is grateful for thofe it receives : both of thefe fhew their bringing up, and reflect honour or difgrace upon thofe who have had the care of their childhood.

As the child approaches to womanhood, it is of the utmoft confequençe, that the parent fhould obtain her friendfhip and confidence, that fhe fhould pour out the moft fecret thoughts of her heart into the bofom of her parent : Where this charming friendfhip is eftablifhed, the maiden will feek for no other confident ; and thus a number of dangers incident to this critical period of life, will be avoided. Here again I refer your Ladyfhip to Madame

K d'Almane,

d'Almane, whofe treatment of her Adelaide is a pattern to all mothers.

I am not a competent judge of the
manners of the great; I can only take
my knowledge from that of others; but
from what has been advanced by the writers of late years, it fhould feem that they
ftand in need of a reformation as much,
if not more than any other degree, becaufe
of the influence they have upon the lower
orders.

Here I beg leave to recommend to
your Ladyfhip two pamphlets, one called
—Thoughts on the Importance of the
Manners of the Great; the other—An
Eftimate of the Religion of the fafhionable World.—They are imputed to a lady
whofe writings have done honour to our
fex, and to human nature, Mrs. Hannah
More.

There is another miftake in the education of the youth of both fexes—that of
putting

putting into their hands books above their years and underftandings; by the reading of thefe, they feem by the partial parents to acquire a prematurity of knowledge, while they are in reality far more ignorant than thofe who advance flowly and furely, whofe underftandings are gradually culti-vated, and whofe reafon is gently affifted, till it attains its full maturity.

If a child is fond of reading, it fhould be indulged with difcretion, and not fuf-fered to hurt its health, or overload its mind. If it has no afpirations after learn-ing, it fhould never be compelled to read more than duty requires. The preceptor, or governefs, fhould watch over the facul-ties of the mind as they unfold them-felves, and give them a free and proper direction.

It is not neceffary for women to be doctors of theology, profeffors of arts and fciences, or philofophers. There is a de-

gree

gree of knowledge that may become every ftation in life; but there is a line of beauty in this, as in every thing elfe, and all beyond it is curvature and deformity.

There is a kind of defultory reading that has a tendency to render young people pert and opiniated, vain of a fuperficial knowledge of a few things that every body knows as well as themfelves: but true knowledge makes them modeft and humble.

" A little learning is a dangerous thing;
" Drink deep, or tafte not the Pierian fpring.
" There fhallow drafts intoxicate the brain,
" And largely drinking fobers us again."

POPE.

It is incumbent on all parents, guardians, and perceptors, to give young people a tafte for good reading, to let them read nothing but what is excellent of its kind, and by thus forming their tafte, to teach them to defpife paltry books of every kind. When they come to maturity,

turity, they will of courſe aſpire to read the beſt, and throw aſide all others.

I * ſend encloſed a liſt of the books I recommended to Miſs Beliza Haughton, as proper for young ladies growing up to womanhood. Your Ladyſhip will give me your opinion of them, and ſelect ſuch as may be uſeful to your young ladies, when they are of years to comprehend them. For this time I will take my leave, being always your Ladyſhip's moſt obedient ſervant,

FRANCES DARNFORD.

* See School for Widows, Vol. II, Page 42.

LETTER

LETTER XVIII.

IF the manners of a nation depend on the education of its youth, and if the prosperity of a nation depends on its virtue, surely it must be the duty of those who assume the title of parents of their people, and take to themselves at least a fourth part of their property to secure to them the remainder, to found, to protect, maintain, and preside over seminaries of education; this office confers more real glory than that of conquerors and warriors, destroyers of mankind.

Among those who have obtained honour of this kind, I will first speak of Madame de Maintenon, the undoubted wife of Louis XIV. She had the spirit, though not the title of a queen, and fulfilled all the duties of that elevated station; but she had been educated.

educated in the school of adversity, which proves and confirms all the virtues of the heart. As soon as she had taken possession of her estate of Maintenon, she erected a school there for female children, and appointed Madame de Brinon to preside over it. From thence they were removed to Ruel, where she increased the number of her adopted children to sixty, and while they remained there they were increased to an hundred; thus was Maintenon the cradle of Saint Cyr.

Madame de Maintenon went often to Ruel, to observe what progress her children made in their education; she took pleasure in teaching and catechising them herself. Her success induced her to bring nearer to her a school, for which her affection increased every day.

The King gave her Noisy; he laid out ten thousand crowns to put it into repair, and prepare it for its new inhabitants.

In this community the ranks were confounded; fome were daughters of the nobleffe, others of tradefmen and merchants,
but all poor and friendlefs.—Madame de
Maintenon was defirous that the peafants
on her lands fhould partake of the benefits
of this eftablifhment. She compofed a body
of their daughters, which fhe called the
daughters of charity, or the blue girls.

They were placed in a lodge on the
outfide of the caftle, and inftruƈted fepa-
rately, fuitably to their birth and deftination. Madame de Maintenon vifited her
principal feminary every day; fhe employed herfelf in the claffes, fhe vifited
the fick, fhe frequently dined with them,
and ate of the fame provifions.

The extreme fondnefs which Madame
de Maintenon difcovered for this Community made the ladies of the Court defirous to fee it; all that went thither admired
and applauded.

The

The King's curiosity was excited by what he heard : he went to Noisy, with all his courtiers : they admired and praised every thing they saw, with as much freedom as if the King had not been present.—From that time the petitions from the officers and placemen were sent to Madame de Maintenon; she received their daughters into her care, and the King settled a fund for paying their pensions to Madame de Brinon.

The report of this establishment spread over all the provinces. Madame de Maintenon was solicited on all sides.—She was so moved with the poverty of the Noblesse, and the sight of their children, which were presented to her, that she sold her jewels, and every thing of value she possessed, to support them. She received as many as she could possibly maintain, and never refused any without the greatest pain to herself. To snatch

K 5

from

from the dangers of the world young
girls of beauty and poverty, was her moſt
favourite charity.

The more good Madame de Maintenon
did, the more ſhe aſpired to do : her exalted mind expanded ſtill wider ; ſhe
was penetrated with the diſtreſſes of the
Nobleſſe, and wiſhed to provide for their
children. Her compaſſion made her break
through a rule ſhe had preſcribed to herſelf of never demanding any thing of the
King.—On this occaſion ſhe repreſented
to him the poverty and diſtreſſes of the
Nobleſſe. She told him, that as a Chriſ-
tian, it was his duty to relieve the unfortunate, and as the King and father of
his country, he was obliged to ſuccour
thoſe families, of which the heads had
ſhed their blood in his ſervice, and thoſe
men whoſe children were ardently deſir-
ous of offering their ſervices to him, de-
preſſed by poverty, and unable to provide

for

for their families. She reprefented thefe
things with fo much energy, that the King
was affected ; he examined into the truth
of them ; he enquired into the fituation
of the Nobleffe in the provinces, and was
ftruck with aftonifhment at the accounts
of their poverty.

Madame de Maintenon was attentive to
the workings of the King's mind ; her
fuperior underftanding made her take the
advantage of thofe times that were favour-
able to her defigns. She fhewed him the
advantages the ftate would receive from
the eftablifhment which fhe had already
begun, and wifhed to extend, and bring
to perfection ; that a good education
would perpetuate virtue and honour in
families, and bind the Nobility to him
by the ftrongeft ties of duty and gratitude.

The King was ftruck with her reafoning ; he took it into ferious confideration ;

he

he was even defirous of improving upon Madame's plan. He propofed a foundation for five hundred young girls of family. The Marquis de Louvois was terrified at the expence, and Madame de Maintenon at the difficulty of educating fo many. They reduced the number to two hundred and fifty girls, thirty-fix ladies to be profeffed, and twenty-four lay fifters. Madame de Maintenon entered into the moft minute particulars of the expence ; fhe held a mean between the extreme of abundance and the extreme of frugality, and traced the plan of utility and eafe, without fuperfluities. After much confultation, the plan was completed. Saint Cyr was fixed upon as the place. The architects were chofen, and the building was begun. Upwards of two thoufand workmen were employed in it, and in eighteen months the building was completed ; within a year afterwards it was fully inhabited.

The

The regulations and ordinances of St. Cyr, were the admiration of all Europe. The pope defired to have a copy of them.

The edict of erection regiftered in the parliament, June 1686, does more honour to the memory of Louis XIV, than all the reft of his actions. The trophies of vain-glory, ftatues, and infcriptions, turn their memory into ridicule and burlefqne, but their good actions are immortal. The enemies of kings fpeak of them only as tyrants. Mr Paine has fpoken of Louis XIV, as a mere player, " acting the ftage tricks and pageantry of royalty ;" but let us view him in another light, educated in the lap of indolence and luxury, idolifed by his people, flattered by his courtiers, render proud, vain-glorious and arbitrary. Then view him humbled by a fucceffion of misfortunes, convinced of his errors, penitent for his crimes, ardently

dently defirous to make attonement for them, and at laft becoming really the father of his people, the object of their refpect and veneration. Once when Madame de Maintenon was fpeaking to him of the good effects of the education at St. Cyr, he anfwered, " O that I could give to God as many fouls as my bad example has fnatched from him !

His laft words to his fucceffor prove his fincere repentance. " I have been " too fond of war ; fhun my example, and " endeavour to live in peace with your " neighbours. In all your actions have " in view the glory of God, and the good " of your people ; love them, and they " will honour you. I am grieved for " the condition I leave them in. Endea- " vour to leffen the taxes, and do what " I have been fo unhappy as not to have " done."

This account of the origin and efta-

blifhment

blifhment of St. Cyr, is extracted from
The Memoirs of Madame de Maintenon ;
here I fhall conclude this letter, remaining always, 　　　Madam,

　　　　　Your faithful fervant,

　　　　　　　FRANCES DARNFORD.

LETTER

LETTER XIX.

MRS. DARNFORD TO LADY A————.

WILL you, my dear Lady, permit me to add a little more to what I have said upon St. Cyr?—The King gave a brevet to Madame de Maintenon, by which he invested her with all the rights, honours, and prerogatives of Foundress of St. Cyr.

The Bishop of Chartres declared by an ordinance, that it was the King's will and pleasure, that Madame de Maintenon should be perpetual Superior of this Community; which was called the Community of St. Louis.—The Ladies of St Louis sent her a gold cross, adorned with fleurs de lys, with two verses of Racine enngraved upon it:

> " Elle est notre guide fidelle,
> " Notre felicité vient d'elle."

This

This truly royal inftitution was, in its childhood, in danger of being overthrown by fome unforefeen accidents.—Madame de Brinon, whom Madame de Maintenon appointed her fubftitute as Superior to the Community, difappointed her hopes in the government of it. She was a woman of fuperior abilities, and took a fhare in compofing the regulations. When fhe found herfelf at the head of the Community, honoured by the friendfhip of Madame de Maintenon, praifed by the King, flattered by her dependants, fhe became intoxicated by thefe honours, and her head was completely turned. She af-fumed the ftile and manners of a princefs, and demanded the fame honours as her pa-tronefs. She made herfelf ridiculous and contemptible, and it was found neceffary to remove her.

This event gave great concern to Ma-dame de Maintenon; however, nothing could

could interfere with the good of the community; fhe fettled a penfion on Madame de Brinon, and continued her favour and protection to the end of her life.

The fecond danger to the community, was the introduction of fanaticifm, by the famous Madame de Guion.

Fanaticifm feized on the imaginations of the Ladies of St. Cyr; Madame Guion had dreams, vifions, and revelations; fhe preached, prayed, and prophefied; fhe was beautiful and eloquent; her doctrines infinuated themfelves into the hearts of her hearers; moft of them were infpired alfo; even the Foundrefs was infected; feveral ladies of the firft quality caught this mania; but the moft extraordinary pupil of Madame Guion, was the great, the fublime Fenelon, whom fhe called her Son in the Lord.

The Clergy, at length, took the alarm; they examined the doctrines of Madame

Guion;

Guion; they were divided in opinion; however, they agreed in perfecuting the Lady, and cenfuring her hearers. They obliged the Ladies of St. Cyr to give up all her writings.—Madame de Maintenon gave up her books to the Bifhop of Chartres, before the whole Community; the reft followed her example, but with extreme reluctance; it was a long while before the effects were worn out at St. Cyr.

The Bifhops perfecuted Fenelon; they carried their complaints to Rome; the Pope and his Council differed in opinion concerning his maxims of the faints.—Infallibility was perplexed; it was at laft obliged to condemn this book. Fenelon himfelf condemned it; he read his recantation in his own church. All France was in confufion, and it was a long time before this ferment fubfided, and peace in the church was reftored. In the mean time St. Cyr was fully eftablifhed, and its

reputation

reputation fpread through all Europe, as the moft perfect inftitution of its kind.

It was imitated by feveral other Princes. The Queen of Sweden, fifter of Charles XII. endeavoured to raife a community fomething like it; but Sweden was fo ex-haufted by the wars of the late King, and the fenate laid fo many reftraints upon the reigning Prince, that fhe was obliged to give it up.

The prefent Emprefs of Ruffia has founded an eftablifhment that in many re-fpects refembles it. It is upon a larger fcale; five hundred pupils are maintained in it.

Louis XIV. had declared at the firft eftablifhment of St. Cyr,—" There are " Convents enough already; I will found " a Community, and not a Convent."— This was evidently his intention, but after the ecclefiaftics interfered, they did not let him reft till they had carried all their

points;

points; they perfuaded him, that it was neceffary for its well doing, that it fhould be a Convent ; and at laft the King confented to their importunities, and it became a Convent; however, it ftill maintained its reputation as a feminary of education.

I fhould be glad to know what the new Conftitution has done with refpect to St. Cyr. The firft reformers in England and Scotland were violent in their proceedings ; they deftroyed many good as well as bad eftablifhments. After things were fettled, they returned to a better temper and a more tolerating fpirit. I believe and hope it will be fo in France. The National Affembly had many injuries to redrefs, many evils to fubdue, many errors to reform. Whether or no they have gone too far, time and experience only can decide. I have contended for a fubordination of ranks and degrees of men, but the kind of fubſubordination I defend, is confiſtent with the moſt perfect liberty that mankind are capable of enjoying.

ʼThere muſt be a form of government, there muſt be governors.—There muſt be laws, to which both the governing, and the governed, muſt ſubmit, and be re-ſtrained by them.—Deſpotic Princes have in the end deſtroyed the baſis upon which they ſtood; they have ſhewn to the people that they may be free, whenever they are unanimous.

The Revolution in France will be a ſtanding leſſon to Princes and to People of all countries; it is a warning to Kings, how they oppreſs and impoveriſh their people; it warns them to reform the errors and corruptions of their governments, and to prevent the neceſſity of a revolution.

I think there ought to be a ſubordina-tion of rank preſerved; there has always

been

been in the freeft countries. Rome in her republican ftate, admitted thefe degrees of fubordination ;—the Patricians, the Equites, the Plebeians : befide thefe, there was a gradation in the public offices, that anfwered all the purpofes of more minute divifions and diftinctions. The Nobility of France were the caufe of her greateft grievances and oppreffions ;—they wanted to be limited and regulated, inftead of that they are annihilated. Whether this be a wife meafure, time muft fhow : however, this alfo may be a warning to other ftates not to increafe too far the number of the nobility, nor to extend their privileges.

St. Cyr cannot be preferved upon her former foundations ; thofe who have annihilated nobility, will not educate their children; but it will do honour to its founders, as long as it ftands on the records of hiftory, and be a model for the imitation of Princes.

Though the power of founding fuch

Com-

Communities, lies only in the great and the rich, yet people of all degrees may imitate them, according to their abilities, may contribute their fhare to the public utility, and to the relief of individuals, and have an equal merit with thofe whofe power is more extenfive.

Madame di Soranzo wifhes to found fuch a Community as I have defcribed, upon a leffer fcale, and place me at the head of it.

Mrs. Strictland reafons againft it, and when fhe has tired herfelf, laughs us out of it. The truth is, fhe is unwilling to part with us, and fears our putting this fcheme into execution.

In the mean time fhe is fcheming herfelf, and engages us in the fuccefs of her plan, in preference to ours. She intends to found a School of Induftry, and to eftablifh a manufactory in her own village. —She has engaged Mr. and Mrs. Elton,

Mr.

Mr. James Balderſon, Mr. Southgate, Madame di Soranzo, and myſelf. We are to ſubſcribe a ſum yearly, till the undertaking can go alone, which, we hope, will be in a few years. She is Generoſity perſonified, as you already know by the memoirs of the Marney family.

My paper warns me to finiſh this letter.

I am, dear Lady A——,

Yours faithfully,

FRANCES DARNFORD.

LETTER

LETTER XX.

MRS. DARNFORD TO LADY A——.

LADY A—— defires that I will conclude my plans, and my remarks
upon them. Lord A—— defires to know
my opinions on the education of boys;
particularly on the great queftion yet undecided, whether a public or private education is the beft.

I have completed the firft part of my
defign; as to the fecond, I dare not prefume to decide the important queftion.

" Who fhall decide when doctors difagree,
" And *female* cafuifts doubt like you and me?"

PoPE.

There have been fo many that have
written upon this fubject, there is fo much
to be faid on both fides, that I cannot even
judge for myfelf, but remain in doubt.
Perhaps a public education may be beft

for

for fome difpofitions—a private one for others. Some have faid, that a public education is moft likely to produce eminent men—a private, virtuous ones ; even this will bear a difpute, as the inftances we fee to the contrary, refutes all this kind of reafoning.

Mr. Cumberland in his Obferver, gives inftances of both kinds of education, and decides in favour of a public education. That it enlarges the mind in fome refpects, I believe, but it may expand too much, and be as ready to receive impreffions of vice, as of virtue :—of the former it fees too much, and may grow fo familiarifed to it, as to think it no crime.

I knew two youths educated at St. Paul's School---the one was vicious to a degree that ruined his conftitution, the other virtuous in an equal degree, and ardently folicitous to reclaim his friend; they both flept in the fame houfe with a friend of

L 2 mine,

mine. The good lad was fubject to talk in his fleep, and frequently brought all the family to his chamber door, fuppofing that fomething more than common had happened to him. His honeft mind was fo full of his concern for his friend, that he gave him in his fleep, a lecture that would have done honour to a man twice his age. He quoted Juvenal, Horace, Virgil, and the reft of the ancients. He quoted Shakefpeare and Rowe; he recited feveral hundred verfes of various authors; he paufed, hemmed, fetched his breath, and went on again, all the time in the moft profound fleep; but his good heart appeared in all that he faid. This inftance of my own knowledge (for the good lad is at this hour living, and a good man in every fenfe of the word), proves that variety of characters are formed by the fame mode of education; even among children

born

born of the fame parents, and brought up under the fame roof, this diverfity of cha-racters is to be found. What is the caufe of this diverfity? Is it organization? We are told that there are no innate ideas; but perhaps there may be innate propenfities, which will come to nearly the fame thing. Perhaps the all-wife creator has willed, that the fame variety fhould be in the minds of his creatures, as is feen in their counte-nances; but you will fay, all this is only conjecture; very true; and I am inclined to believe that all abftrufe reafoning is the fame. It is for this reafon that I wifh to fimplify every fubject, and to bring it as near as poffible to the ftandard of common fenfe. Upon this ground only we can ftand firmly, and here let us reft our feet. To infift upon implicit obedience during the ftate of infancy, and the firft ftages of childhood; to inculcate early

L 3 habits

habits of doing right things, and avoiding wrong ones; to lay the firſt principles of piety, modeſty, ſobriety, frugality, induſtry, prudence, and an abhorrence of vices of every kind. In theſe there can be no miſtake, and upon this foundation you may build every accompliſhment, without injury to the principles. In the letters imputed to Pope Ganganelli (it is no matter whether they were written by him or another man), there is an excellent one upon the ſubjeƈt of education; I will only tranſcribe a few paſſages, and recommend the whole to your peruſal.

" There are many reaſons for adviſing a domeſtic " education, and there are ſtill more which hinder me " from perſuading you to it. Domeſtic education is " commonly the beſt calculated to ſecure their morals; " but it preſents ſuch a ſameneſs, it is ſo lukewarm, " and languid, that it diſcourages all emulation; be- " ſides this, as they are watched too narrowly, they " are more likely to become hypocrites than good " pupils.

" Nevertheleſs, if you can find a preceptor gentle, " patient, ſociable, and learned, who can unite conde- " ſcenſion with ſteadineſs, wiſdom with gaiety, temper-

" ance

" ance with amiablenefs, 1 fhould defire you to make
" the trial; being perfuaded that you will do nothing
" but in concert with him, and that you will not feek
" to controul him. There are too many fathers who
" look upon a preceptor as a mercenary, and illibe-
" rally think they are his mafters, becaufe he receives
" a falary from them.

" Truft your fons only to a man upon whom you can
" depend as upon yourfelf; but after you have found
" fuch a man, do not hefitate to leave them entirely to
" his difpofal. Nothing difgufts a governor fo much
" as diftruft, and a diffidence of his capacity. Take
" care what fervants you admit about your children,
" for it is generally through them that youth are
" corrupted."

GANGANELLI'S LETTERS, Vol. II.

The author of thefe letters feems doubtful which method to prefer, but upon the
whole, feems to recommend a preceptor.
I fhall here conclude what I intended to
fay upon the fubject, unlefs you fhould
afk my opinion upon any particular point
relative to the education of individuals.

I am now preparing for my journey to
London, where I fhall hope to converfe
with you face to face, and to pay my ac-

knowledgements for your favours con-
ferred upon, Madam,

      Your moſt obliged friend,

          and faithful ſervant,

            FRANCES DARNFORD.

LETTER

LETTER XXI.

MRS. DARNFORD TO MRS. STRICTLAND.

London, Feb. 20.

MY DEAR FRIEND;

MY firſt letter gave you an account of our ſafe arrival in London, and of our hoſpitable reception from Mrs. Langſton; my preſent will tell you things of more conſequence.—Mr. Maurice arrived here fifteen days before us; he called every day, but we did not admit him till two days after our arrival. He ſeemed impatient to ſee us; he bowed to me, and then fixed his eyes upon Charlotte; he embraced her fervently: the dear girl was offended at the liberty; ſhe bluſhed, and retired backwards. He then ſaluted me; he was ſilent for ſome minutes, looking upon Charlotte and me alternately; his eyes run over, his breaſt heaved, and it was ſome minutes before he could ſpeak. At

L 5 length

length he fpoke—" What can I fay, what
" can I do, to fhew my gratitude to you,
" Madam !—My friend, my comforter,
" my guardian angel !" " Compofe your-
" felf, Sir; I fee your heart without any dif-
" guife; it is fenfible and grateful; thank
" God that I have been enabled to ferve
" you in the perfons moft dear to you !"
—" Oh, Madam, fuffer me to fpeak the
" fulnefs of my heart !—you have cured
" it of all its anguifh, and reftored me
" to peace and tranquillity.—My fweet
" child !—how fhe is grown, how much
" improved ! I hope fhe is fenfible of
" her obligations to you ?" " She is, Sir:
" but will you give me leave to tell her
" of thofe fhe owes to you ?"—" As you
" pleafe, Madam ; I will do whatever you
" think proper." " Charlotte, my dear,
" kneel to that gentleman, and afk his
" bleffing; he is your father, and you are
" wholly at his difpofal."—She burft into

tears ;

tears; fhe kneeled to him, and kiffed his hand.—He embraced, and wept over her. —" Oh that thy mother was living, to fee " this day!—But fhe is a faint in heaven; " and I wrong her to wifh her in this bad " world.—This lady has well fupplied her " place to you, and done more for you " than fhe could have done; you can " never be too grateful to her."——

Charlotte acknowled her obligations to me in a very pretty and engaging manner; adding—" I hope, Sir, you will not take " me away from Mrs. Darnford?"—— " Not as long as fhe is willing to take the " charge of you," he faid. I made them both eafy on this head; he grew compofed, and we talked of other fubjects.

I took occafion to fend Charlotte to fit with Mrs. Langfton, and then we entered upon the fituation of Madame di Soranzo. He was unbounded in his acknowledgements to me upon her account, and de-

L 6

fired

fired to know what farther fhe required of him. I told him, that fhe was defirous to fell her eftate at D——, and that fhe and I had engaged to live together, and to hire a houfe in a diftant village, near a very dear friend of mine; that we requefted him to fign an inftrument, by which he gave up all claim upon the property of Madame di Soranzo, and acknowledged that he was not her hufband.

He was willing to do the firft, but very reluctant to do the laft, as he thought it would expofe his conduct towards her. I told him, this inftrument fhould not be fhown to any one but the perfon who fhould purchafe Madame di Soranzo's eftate; and I would undertake that it fhould not be explained to his difadvantage, but only, as he was the perfon who took care of her affairs, while fhe was incapable of attending to them, that reports had gone forth, that they were married, which he had not

contra-

contradicted at that time, nor till it became neceffary, to enable her to difpofe of her eftate. We argued this point for fome time, but at laft he gave it up handfomely, faying, he could not deny me any thing. Charlotte came down to drink tea with us, and our vifitor went away foon after, well fatisfied with us both.

The man is fenfible, and has a feeling heart; and however aukwardly he has been fituated, is not a bad man. I am defirous to think the beft of him for Charlotte's fake, to whom he is an affectionate father, and deferves her duty and affection.

I have received a letter from Lady A——; the family will come to town next week, fomewhat the fooner on my account.

It will be painful to me to fee Lord A——, but for his Lady's fake I will fee him; but I will not be too much acquainted with him. His confeffion to his Lady was

an

an ungenerous one; he told the truth, *but not all the truth*. She knows not the worſt part of his conduct towards me, and I hope ſhe never will; from me ſhe ſhall not. It has been ſaid, The man who marries, gives hoſtages to the public for his good behaviour: upon that, and my Lady's friendſhip for me, I ſhall rely. I ſhall neither ſeek nor avoid his company; and if his behaviour is not to my liking, I ſhall ſhorten my ſtay in town.

Mrs. Langſton is in ill health, but, I think, in no preſent danger. She has urged me warmly to make her houſe my home; but I have told her my engagement to Madame di Soranzo. She is un-willing to be convinced of the neceſſity of my compliance with it; but you know, that when I think I am doing right, I can be firm and ſteady: I am ſo in the preſent caſe.

I want to perſuade Mrs. Langſton to
take

take fome unfortunate gentlewoman to be her companion and houfekeeper. If I can meet with fuch an one, I fhall urge it to her : but *entre nous*, was I difengaged, I would not be the perfon myfelf. She has neither the mind nor the temper I fhould require, in the perfon in whofe hands I muft truft my own peace and comfort.

I will call on my fifter in the city, and try whether fhe will acknowledge me, and fpeak to me kindly ; my heart yearns towards her.—Why muft I be the leaft beloved by all thofe who are neareft, and fhould be deareft to me ?—But hufhed be this complaint, and all repining thoughts; have I not found friends where-ever I have fet my foot ?—Among all of them, not one is fo dear to my heart, as her to whom my pen now fpeaks, and tells her I am truly hers,

F. DARNFORD.

LETTER

LETTER XXII.

MRS. DARNFORD TO MRS. STRICTLAND.

London, Feb. 28.

CAPTAIN MAURICE has called here almoft every day fince my laft. He converfes with eafe and freedom ; and though not a man of polifhed manners, he has a general kind of knowledge, and is by no means difagreeable. He has figned the inftrument which I prepared for him, trufting in me, that I would make no ill ufe of it ; he did it in a very handfome manner.

He has fince done a generous action ; for the firft was only an act of juftice.— He has added to Charlotte's fortune, in prefents ; it is now full three thoufand pounds. He makes me her guardian; and fhe is to receive her fortune when fhe

comes

comes of age; or if she marries sooner, with my consent, (upon which, he says, his depends) upon the day of her marriage.

After this was accepted, he took another paper out of his pocket, and bowing very low, offered it to me. I desired to know the contents, otherwise I could not accept it.—He blushed—hesitated—and looked as if soliciting a favour, rather than confering one. This is the criterion of true generosity; it is not confined to pecuniary matters; it is modest, diffident, humble—in short—it is greatness of soul! Monsieur St. Evremond says, that most of those people who complain of ingratitude, ought rather to be complained of.—They know not how to confer favours; they humble the receiver to dust, and then complain of ingratitude.—If people knew how to confer them, there would be few persons ungrateful. Maurice

rice declined opening the paper; I returned it to him. He then fpoke with
fome confufion, as follows :—

"My obligations to you, Madam, are
"fuch as I can never repay. Firft, you
"have reftored my mind to peace with
"itfelf, by recovering Donna Ifabella to
"health of mind and body; and fecond-
"ly, you have been a mother to my
"child, and you will continue your
"cares for her, till fhe is of an age to act
"for herfelf.—I humbly beg your ac-
"ceptance of my beft acknowledgements,
"and of an act and deed which proves
"my gratitude for your great and real
"fervices to me and mine. This paper
"is an act of fettlement of my farm at
"D——, upon my Charlotte, irrevo-
"cably; and the income of it to you,
"Madam, during your life."

I was aftonifhed and confounded.—I
declined accepting it. He kneeled to me,
and

and with tears in his eyes befought me,
for his own peace and happinefs, to accept
his honeft and fincere gratitude.—I was
diftreffed ; he was refolute ; and he gained
the victory.

Charlotte ran into my arms, and thanked
me for obliging her father ; in fhort, we
we were all fo much affected, that we did
not foon recover it ; as foon as Mr. Maurice was compofed, he left us.

The next day he called again ; he looked more chearful than I ever faw him.—
" Madam," faid he, " I flept well laft
" night, and am happier than I have been
" for many years paft ; I thank God, and
" I thank you !"—" I rejoice to hear
" you fay fo, Sir ; may the remainder of
" your days be eafy and happy !"——
" Thank you again and again, Madam ;
" and may you be rewarded for all your
" goodnefs !"

After fome further converfation, he defired

fired to fpeak with me alone. — When
Charlotte left us, he feemed in confufion;
after fome paufe, he faid, " I muft afk
" you a queftion, Madam, that will de-
" cide the fate of my future days?"—
" Proceed, Sir."—After another paufe—
" Do you think that Donna Ifabella is
" convinced of my penitence, and that
" fhe forgives my paft conduct?"—" She
" does, I am certain."—" Do you think
" that I might form any hope, that fhe
" would ever accept of me for a hufband?"
—" No, Sir; you have no reafon to hope
" that fhe will ever. She is wedded to
" the memory of her hufband; and was
" fhe in her own country, fhe would re-
" tire into a religious houfe for the reft
" of her life. My fervices have given
" me fome influence with her, and fhe is
" fo much attached to me, that fhe and
" I have promifed to live always toge-
" ther."

" And

" And have both of you refolved
" never to marry again ?"—" We have,
" Sir; and I believe our refolutions can-
" not be fhaken."

He fighed, and paufed for fome minutes; after which,—" Madam, I will
" open my heart to you. I have been a
" wanderer all my life; I wifh to be a
" fettled man, and to have fomebody
" to love me, and take care of me all
" the latter days of my life."—" A very
" rational wifh, Sir, and a very reafonable
" one."—" There is a lady in Rotter-
" dam, the widow of a fhip-mafter, a
" perfon in my own line of life. I have
" been wifhed to offer myfelf to her, and
" told that fhe would not refufe me. I
" determined to fee what England would
" do for me firft; but if thofe I fhould
" like beft, refufe me, I don't fee that I
" ought to condemn myfelf to a life of
" folitude."

" Very

" Very true, Sir; you are very much
" in the right. I would advife you by
" all means to addrefs the Dutch lady,
" and I heartily wifh you fuccefs."—
" She has a very good fortune, Madam;
" fhe is about forty years of age, and a
" very comely woman."—" So much the
" better, Sir; I wifh you all manner of
" happinefs."

This was the chief part of our converfation. I know that you will be enter-
tained by it; but I will not fuffer you to
laugh at our honeft, generous, Captain
Maurice.

As Charlotte Brady will have fo handfome a fortune, I will give her fome of
the ornamental accomplifhments. She has
already an eminent dancing mafter to attend her; and fhe fhall learn mufic and
drawing, befide; I will fhow her all that
is worth feeing in town, and carry her
once or twice to each of the public places;
teaching

teaching her, at the fame time, to diftinguifh between the tinfel ornaments, and
things of intrinfic value.

Lady A—— is juft come to town, fhe
defires to fee me as foon as poffible; I will
give you an account of my vifit.

Accept and diftribute my regards among
all my friends at Woodlands. I write to
Madame di Soranzo under the fame cover.
For this time I bid you adieu!

F. DARNFORD.

LETTER

LETTER XXIII.

MRS. DARNFORD, TO MRS. STRICTLAND.

London, March, 5.

I HAVE feen Lady A——, my dear friend, and I have feen Lord A—— alfo ; but I know you expect particulars.

I called at their houfe yefterday morning, London ftile, but we fhould have called it afternoon, at Woodlands. Lady A—— received me with that gracioufnefs and affability that are natural to her. She did me the honour to embrace me. We chatted upon the fubjects of our late correfpondence, and the time flew away unperceived. She urged me to ftay to dine with her ; I would have declined it, but ftill fhe infifted. " My Lord dines abroad " to day," faid fhe, " and it would be " cruel of you to leave me alone."—— That confideration had its weight with me, and I complied.

She

She fpoke of reconciling me to her lord.
I expected, and I was prepared for it; I
guarded all I faid with the greateft care;
but kept off as much as poffible. She
prefented her daughters to me, and their
governefs; a fenfible, well behaved young
woman.—The young ladies, well bred
and promifing, in all refpects. Lady A—
told me fhe would fpare the governefs to
you, as foon as I could provide her with
another.

Lady A—— is big with child, as I fuppofed from a fentence in one of her letters; this will increafe my lord's obligations to her, and be a happy cement to
their union.

My lady would not part with me foon;
at about eleven my Lord A—— came in.
—He was embaraffed at the fight of me,
and I faw that he exerted himfelf to over-
come it. He behaved with the utmoft
refpect to me, and with tender attention

M   to

to his lady. I told them I muſt return,
for that Mrs. Langford was an invalid,
and I could not keep her ſervants up.—
My lady ordered the coach ; my lord offered to attend me home ; but that I could
not ſuffer for many reaſons. He would
put me into the coach, and in doing that,
he thanked me for my prudence and generoſity in not expoſing him to his lady.
I repent of my paſt conduct, Madam, and
will deſerve your friendſhip in future ;
whether I am ſo happy as to obtain it or
not.—I did not get home till paſt twelve
o'clock.

I have called on my ſiſter in the city ;
ſhe ſeemed aſtoniſhed to ſee me. She
looked me over. I was dreſſed genteely,
and looked like a perſon eaſy, and freed
from cares of every kind.—She aſked me
whether I was married again ? I anſwered,
—No ; and I believed I never ſhould ;
but I avoided making reſolutions. —
                                    " Who

" Who do you live with, then ?"—I am at prefent on a vifit to Mrs. Langfton, in Clarges-ftreet, Piccadilly ; but I have taken a houfe in the village where Mrs. Strictland lives, formerly Mifs Selwyn ; and I hope in a fhort time to be fettled there."—" What then is become of the mad woman with whom you lived ?"— " That *lady* is reftored to health and tranquillity ; fhe and I have engaged to live together during our lives."—" I am glad to hear that you are in eafy circumftances ?" —" Perfectly fo ; 1 am as rich as I ever defire to be, and as happy as I wifh to be ; I could not be in London, without calling upon my fifter, and énquiring after the health of herfelf and family." — She changed her tone ; became civil and converfible ; but never afked me to fpend a day with her while I ftaid in town. I have done my duty, and am quite eafy about her.

I am

I am refolved to fettle a thoufand pounds upon Patty Martin, and then I fhall have difcharged my duty towards her.

When all my bufinefs is done, I fhall return to you with a heart at eafe, and as blythe as a lark.

I will never be without a purfuit; bufinefs employs the mind, and keeps life from ftagnating.

Adieu, my dear friend.

I am always yours, faithfully,

FRANCES DARNFORD.

F I N I S.